Quality is never an accident. It is always the result of intelligent effort.

John Ruskin

SELECTED WORKS
2006–2016

COOL + CONTEMPORARY + CLASSIC
A DESIGN MANIFESTO

JULIE HUMPHRYES AND DAVID ARCHER

Modern architecture is often defined by its opposition to interior design. Architects like to consider themselves as serious and philosophical, understanding materials and space at a higher conceptual level than interior designers who, they may think, are often untrained and merely deal in mood and decoration.

This is a novel division in a profession that until relatively recently has been involved with all aspects of the built environment. From ancient civilisations right through to Michelangelo, Robert Adam and Le Corbusier, any division between architecture and interior design in the execution of conceptual ideals was out of the question. Except for the most artificial theorising or the most detailed contemplation, it is impossible to experience a building purely as a structure whose interior is not inhabited, and it is equally impossible to conceive of an interior that does not relate to the structure framing it.

Separation of the two disciplines of architecture and design is symptomatic of a wider dislocation affecting all aspects of contemporary endeavour. As both technology and knowledge become more accessible and more complex, our projects accrete an ever greater number of experts and stakeholders with an ever narrower focus. A key aspect of design today lies in engaging with the complexity of process that this crowded landscape of disciplines, experts and professions has created. A strong design will be informed and strengthened by its engagement with this cacophony of voices. But a weak design will be consumed or enlisted to another purpose, much in the way that a computer virus overpowers and co-opts weak coding.

One of the keys to overcoming the threats posed by specialisation is to focus on the experienced or 'felt' environment in a way that modern cerebral architecture finds difficult to express, but which interior designers and more classical architects have not. Rather than striving for physical statements, Archer Humphryes Architects explores architecture as a way of influencing how people respond and behave within spaces. What follows is a set of principles for practicing contemporary architecture in this way. While not all these can be adopted all of the time, we have aspired to them in the projects that follow in this book.

COOL

Function is often said to define form. An airport must look like an airport and a museum must look like a museum. Cool, however, is something that is a sensation rather than a thought. It is mutable and is inherently playful with function. Emotion and feeling need to be acknowledged as a key part of design. Even if not cool, buildings should be loved, unorthodox, or awe-inspiring rather than simply functional.

Colour is key to defining mood and therefore central to cool architecture. Although hugely important in setting scenes, it is rarely discussed as a subject of serious enquiry in architectural language, and often only enters into the equation far into the design process. Colours are always agreed with a client at the outset and the design evolves accordingly.

Texture, like colour, is a crucial determinant of spatial character and the integrity of structural composition. Materials and surfaces should be determined early on, preferably ahead of form and layout. There would be nothing wrong with creating intensity by consciously designing a whole space around a particular material. Igloos, a glass skyscraper, the Casa Grande are all derived from mastery of a singular material choice.

Light, sound and other sensed and felt elements also need to be given prominence as drivers of a project's overall design theme. The manner in which these elements are combined from one project to another and even the mix of the elements themselves must constantly evolve. The first ice hotel could not be anything other than cool, for example, but the second, the third and the fourth inevitably have an ever-stronger affinity with the commonplace.

Cool must be recognisably outside of the mundane and not follow the tedium of repetitiousness, but equally should not be an affront. Surrealism or extreme radicalism that seeks to provoke feelings of shock and disgust cannot ever be cool. Successful cool architecture should rather encourage a life just beyond the ordinary, one that a person entering the space for the first time aspires to but which has hitherto been out of reach or not articulated. The development of cool architecture therefore requires engagement and differentiation rather than a conscious reach for the surreal or bizarre. Setting out to create a pre-packaged, signature style ultimately results in sterile, unoriginal thinking and lacklustre, stereotypical and lackadaisical solutions.

While at any given moment it is easy to point out something which is cool, and something which is not, coolness nevertheless eludes definition. As there is no universal understanding of what constitutes a cool building, it should not be the absolute pursuit of the designer to achieve this. Instead, what is cool is determined in the mind of the audience.

What is clear however is that cool changes over time, and from place to place. It is also true that what is cool for one person may not be cool for another. In any finished project, cool must therefore be felt by as many as possible of the people who engage with it. In architecture, cool is something that must be imparted by the designer creatively in their flare for imagining three-dimensional space. In creating a destination and a place, the architect does not set out to 'be cool'—they enjoy the adventure of what they are participating in with like-minded people who want to achieve the unthinkable with vigorous endeavour. The resultant architecture must not be a hollow statement devoid of human and interior participation.

CONTEMPORARY

Arriving at an image of cool architecture in practice is the richest and most challenging element of contemporary practice. The development and completion of any new project is a dialectical process of increasing complexity. The number of stakeholders seems to continually multiply and the rules, guidelines, science and other agendas driving them continually expands and deepens. Planners to plumbers to PR consultants to pathogen control technicians, futurologists, heritage consultants, mood managers, and diverse regulators are just a small number of the parties that a classical architect such as Robert Adam would not have encountered or, necessarily, listened to. The successful modern project must however mature and develop through its engagement with these parties and its embodiment of their requirements in agreed, and often negotiated, form. Design by committee can lead to splintered thinking and disrupt the design process. It therefore takes steadfast vision to conceive a building by juxtaposing design disciplines with an increasing responsibility for exacting budgets and governing bodies. By wading through such immense noise, you can only arrive at a contemporary architecture by being unwavering in the face of pessimistic inputs.

The built and natural environment that a project inhabits is more significant than the articulated combined views of stakeholders. The conservationist, the urban planner or the ecological activist for example approaches the project disjointedly and responds to the environment with a particular philosophy and agenda that does not necessarily prioritise the tenets of design. It is the role of the architect to steer the ideas within this cultural context and traverse often disparate expert positions to form cohesion. A strong architect combines a holistic approach to architecture, interiors, furniture and landscape, capturing and intertwining the wider skills and talents of the extended team to create a project exemplar. A weak design arises from not being able to delineate the experts, and surrenders to the architectural thuggery of an indiscriminate design that interrupts the landscape with nothing to contribute to the conversation. A lively, collaborative collegiate-style studio is vital to the success of the design, providing somewhere for the extended team and clients to meet and evolve the design in a direction true to their aims.

Technology equally generates complexity and is vital to the navigation and mastery of the design process. The development of web and video based design tools has permanently altered the means of communicating and developing design. The more immersive and total the representation of a project becomes in all media, the greater the designer's ability to guide the process of development. The effective accumulation and management of data and detail are requirements of successful contemporary design. Conveying ideas and maximising the visual impact of the images produced leads to exchanges and explorations which otherwise remain hidden and excluded from the debate about contemporary architecture.

CLASSIC

Beset by modern complexity, the contemporary architect often imagines a classic past that is defined by simplicity and purity of form and expression. This is an imagined and eclectic tradition. Its masterpieces are sensitive to mood and environment but may contain, at any given moment, an Eames chair, the Palladian villa, the divine proportion or golden ratio, the Mies van der Rohe-designed Seagram Building in New York, a window by Marc Chagall or an eighteenth-century romantic ruin. At another time and place, the list would be entirely different.

The contemporary architect turns to this imagined past as an inspiration for the essential simplicity and clarity of purpose that informs cool and contemporary design. In a world of increasing complexities, the maintenance of a simple and intuitively comprehensible narrative and attitude throughout a designed environment is itself an essential prerequisite of differentiation.

A classical approach yearns for artistic ideas to begin with hand drawn sketches. Such sketches can convey a concept with clarity without being overburdened with excessive detail or information. Time and again hand drawn conceptual sketches inform the development of design and its iteration through multiple layers of technology and procedures. Immediacy is achieved in being able to sketch in situ to explain thoughts, and indicate how the idea is developing in the mind, without the fuss and finite impression of computer drawings.

Spaces must be designed for people to engage with them on both a practical and an emotional level. The ability to harness the potential of each project's provenance and context is what makes each design solution interesting, memorable and enduring. Recognition that space requires integrated interiors derived from classical architecture does not prevent the incorporation of grand architectural gestures. But it does make the contemporary architect suspicious of design driven purely by theoretical, economic or technical agendas. No matter how admired its exterior may be, a new passenger plane built purely to accommodate the maximum number of passengers will not remain cool in the imagination of travellers. This does not prevent projects in which budgetary, political, religious, academic or other agendas are core from being well designed. Such projects are often highly successful and many would be considered classics.

A cool project cannot instantly be a classic project. By definition, while seeking inspiration from the past, a cool designer will not settle for re-creation or restoration for its own sake, or an imitation or parody of history. Similarly, the aspiration for the ineffable and different, which defines cool, means that any project should not instantly be recognisable as classic. Nevertheless, the greatest accolade for a contemporary architect will be for a project, at some unknowable moment in the future, to be considered to have achieved sufficient simplicity and beauty to be a classic in the eyes of another designer. Such a design will therefore have been cool + contemporary + classic.

A double-height 'shed roof' is symbolic of a Long Thai House and has been described as a viking ship. Pendant lamps are arranged atmospherically and low in the room to light each square table.

INTRODUCTION
PAMELA BUXTON

"It looks like gold dripping down from heaven", says David Archer, gazing up at the glorious pendant lighting in the Steinhof asylum church in Vienna. When I accompanied him on a recent visit to the Otto Wagner-designed church, he was clearly revelling in the exquisite Jugendstil decoration, some of which had directly inspired aspects of Archer Humphryes Architects' Sans Souci Hotel elsewhere in the Austrian capital (p 106).

David has identified the church as a source of inspiration for him and the work of Archer Humphryes Architects, the practice he co-founded with Julie Humphryes in 2002. This splendidly rich church, with its mosaics, stained glass and gilding, seems an appropriate touchstone for a practice that celebrates the interior and all the texture and complexity of design that goes with it—from the delight of a bespoke lampshade inspired by the pattern of a kimono cummerbund from Kyoto, as seen at Aaya restaurant (p 178) to the raw texture of a Thai brick, used to good effect at the Naamyaa cafe/restaurant at Angel in north London (p 216).

A lot of architects are a bit sniffy about interiors. Often early works such as the designs of a bar or an exhibition are clearly regarded almost apologetically as stepping stones to the real architectural event— the 'proper' architecture of the new build. But Archer Humphryes has instead made interiors and architecture, together, its focus, embracing the idea of the *Gesamtkunstwerk* total environment with gusto. After all, as Julie points out, while UK architectural education does not currently offer a course that teaches the inside of the building with the same rigour as that of the outside, historically it has often been the best architects—Borromini, Michelangelo—who have produced the most sophisticated interiors.

Archer and Humphryes met when working on the Sanderson Hotel in London for Ian Schrager in 1997, setting up in practice five years later. While there are some notable exceptions, their work is primarily focused on 'lifestyle' spaces to eat, drink, sleep, to see and be seen, whether restaurants, bars, exotic resorts, residences or most notably hotels, which fruitfully combine several of these elements in one. Long-term clients include the restaurateur Alan Yau, for whom Archer Humphryes has designed Hakkasan; the Busaba Eathai chain (p 228) and Naamyaa.

While London, with its status as a cosmopolitan world city, has been a natural main habitat for the practice, Archer and Humphryes' previous work took them further afield. Julie worked for Studio Daniel Libeskind in Berlin and travelled extensively in the Far East, living in Hong Kong, Moscow and Japan for durations. David Archer worked for Philippe Starck in Paris on projects such as the Peninsula Hotel in Hong Kong and Delano Hotel in Miami. Both have client-side experience. David was head of design for AB Hotels in New York working with, among others, Antonio Citterio and Jean Nouvel, while Julie explored industrial, product and architectural patented designs with Virgin Atlantic, collaborating on projects with Airbus and Boeing with Pearson Lloyd and Barber Osgerby in London. More recently, the practice, whilst Julie was co-head of Yoo Studio, oversaw residential and hotel design for a decade with the company set up by Philippe Starck, with Marcel Wanders and Anouska Hempel adding to the team.

The two principals remain keen travellers in the name of research, whether it be exploring the Baroque Winter and Summer Palaces in Vienna while working on the design for a new hotel in the same city, experiencing the romantic ruins of Diocletian's Palace at Split for their proposed Adam Hotel on the Adriatic (p 156), Buddhist temples in Cambodia, or taking a lengthy tour of sights and cuisine in Thailand, Tokyo and Hong Kong, undertaken as research for the Naamyaa cafe in London. Nearer to home, William Burges' lavish Gothic revival rooms at Cardiff Castle have proved an inspiration for Archer Humphryes' recent proposal for the Grade I listed St Pancras Renaissance Hotel and Chambers.

All this historical and cultural richness serves as spring points for new projects. But crucially, while this research gives their work depth and narrative, the eventual designs aim to wear this context lightly. Rather than dragging down the atmosphere with knowing references, their work strives to be of the now. It is not an easy trick to pull off but is one that is essential for the enjoyment and success of the spaces as contemporary twenty-first century venues.

This is particularly the case in historic contexts, such as the Chiltern Firehouse in Marylebone (p 28) and the Great Northern Hotel at King's Cross (p 76). Archer Humphryes, while respecting the original, is by no means attempting some sort of conservation back to an imagined idea of what the past may have been. Always, the focus is on understanding the past but creating somewhere new and relevant to the times. Perhaps this is the intangible architectural patronage that attracts Prime Ministers, former presidents and a host of A-list celebrities to immerse themselves in the spaces they create.

What characterises their work? Above all else, each design must function as a tool to achieve the particular priorities of the clients— whether for commercial success in bars, restaurants or hotels, or for personal enjoyment, such as Harley Place residence in London (p 386). But beyond that, I think it is possible to identify some common, repeated concerns and ideas. For me, what shines through is a relish of texture, materials and craftsmanship and a delight in setting a mood, all combining to create rich interiors full of visual and tactile interest.

There is a tendency to a sense of discovery, grandeur and drama. At Sans Souci Hotel in Vienna, guests enter the hotel through a richly tiled passage full of niches and statues before emerging into the splendour of the circular reception, with its inlaid stone flooring of Klimt marble and antique furniture. At the Great Northern Hotel, chandeliers, mirrored ceilings and a curving pewter bar convey a contemporary take on the

glamorous age of travel in the *Belle Epoque*. Sans Souci's social spaces are a carefully choreographed riot of modern art, mirrors and Baroque and Carlo Mollino chairs. Archer Humphryes is obviously at home with such exuberance, but only employs this approach when it is appropriate. Elsewhere at Sans Souci, the design is toned right down in the more contemplative pool room where swimmers put in the laps beneath a row of relatively simple chandeliers. And in the private setting of Harley Place, the design is warm and restrained with the chief visual interest created by a cantilevered marble-tread staircase which appears as though suspended in air.

Several of the restaurant interiors convey a grotto-like quality, aided by the frequent use of dark walls combined with glowing feature lighting to create an intimate eating ambience. At Busaba Eathai, for example, the walls are dark stained rattan with wooden beams, teak tables and dark slate, while at the Isarn restaurant (p 202), the walls are clad in ebony.

Throughout the practice's work there is a constant delight in the luxury of material and details, whether the curved leather banquettes and hand-blown glass lanterns of the Great Northern Hotel, or the richly inlaid timber flower motif floor at Sans Souci. At Naamyaa, a wall of traditional Thai brick provides an earthy, rustic counterpoint to the array of gleaming golden Buddhas and decorated ceramic tiling found elsewhere in the cafe.

Tactility is a feature of many of the projects in this book. At the Great Northern Hotel, the plumply upholstered banquettes are just asking to be touched, as are the twisting curves of the stair rails in the Print Room and Ink Bar (p 270), created in the Art Deco former *Bournemouth Daily Echo* building. At the Aaya restaurant, the chrysanthemum motifs that are discreetly scoured into timber wall panels in the dining room invite the hand to touch and explore.

Delight in craftsmanship is tangible in their work. Archer Humphryes particularly enjoys collaborating with craftspeople working in the traditional way with drawings and visits to workshops. Collaboration with the master *ébéniste* Fratelli Boffi in Milan has recently led to Archer Humphryes' third furniture collection, following After Adam (p 162) for April 2016. Initially paying homage to the work of the eighteenth-century

Scottish designer Robert Adam, taking symbols and motifs from his interiors but reworking them for today's hotels, restaurants and homes. The result is a collection of chunky dining tables, elegant easy chairs and fluffily upholstered rockers. Here and there is a ram's head motif, an elegantly turned table leg or an exquisite piece of marquetry, but the overall effect is one of contemporary luxury rather than reverent history. Notably, machined brass is delicately inlaid into mahogany creating an exquisite table using traditional artisan skills with a modern twist.

Archer Humphryes' work does not seem precious. Unlike that found in some 'lifestyle' interiors, the practice likes to employ furniture that is comfortable enough to be used and enjoyed, and develops a patina over time. These look like spaces you would want to spend time in.

While the practice is clearly at home with interiors projects —Chiltern Firehouse being a tour de force of new architecture extension—it will soon be spreading its wings with the imminent completion of the Beach Resort (p 350) in Koh Samui, Thailand, the transformation of the 1960s iconic cantilevered Philips Haus by Kurt Schwanzer (formerly Philips HQ) into a residential apartment building in Vienna, turning the former Camden Town Hall into The Standard Hotel and recently Duck and Rice (p 244), a Chinese gastropub in the heart of Soho. This will be followed by the commencement of Archer Humphryes' Diomed Villas in Croatia (p 346), Television Centre Penthouse at White City, a Michelin 3* restaurant in a Portuguese resort and apartments for Go Native in the City of London. And, in its second decade, as well as taking on more of the niche commissions of individual restaurants and hotels with which the practice has made its name, Archer Humphryes would like to move towards projects with more of a public focus, in particular, more scope to handle the complete environment from the interior, to the architecture, to all the furniture and fittings, much as Wagner did at the Steinhof in Vienna that was so inspirational to the architects. But while for Wagner that proved to be the end of his career, there is the feeling that Archer Humphryes is only at the beginning and getting into its stride.

PLACE SETTING
JAN-CARLOS KUCHAREK

Heading to Rome to curate a show on the great visionary architect Étienne-Louis Boullée, architect Stourley Kracklite, the unfortunate protagonist of Peter Greenaway's 1987 film *The Belly of an Architect*, is first encountered on a train 'in flagrante delicto' with his wife. The two are lain in front of their sleeper window, although the director will curiously keep cutting to the deserted cemeteries of the Tuscan 'campagna'—a portent that would otherwise be lost amongst the landscape's countless Cypresses as the train speeds by. In the next scene the portly architect is guest of honour at a lavish dinner held in front of the fountain of the Piazza della Rotonda; behind him Emperor Trajan's magnificent Pantheon—an ancient echo for Boullée's own architecture. A few minutes later he will retire to the bathroom and, while there, inexplicably vomit in a sink—the first evidence of the stomach cancer he has yet to find out he has. Thus, in ten minutes, Greenaway has given us, framed within his architectural tableau, the core functions dictating our time on this earth—culminating in death.

But Rome is no stranger to such theatricality. The financier Agostina Chigi who, in 1506, commissioned Baldassare Peruzzi to build the magnificent Villa Farnesina on the banks of the Tiber, once threw a great banquet for his first son Lorenzo in its garden loggia and famously had all the fine crockery gold and silver cutlery thrown into the river at its conclusion—omitting to tell his guests that fishing nets were stretched out just below its surface. If these stories tell us anything, it is that hospitality is not only a dramatic 'event' in itself, but can act as a temporal 'illusory' space in which aspects of the human condition can be reified. It is also that food is inseparable from its physical context; the *New Yorker*'s noted culinary critic AJ Liebling once remarked, "A good appetite gives an eater room to turn around in."[1] What he is acknowledging is the fact that the human experience of dining embodies both the meal and the space. It is this key observation that is at the heart of Archer Humphryes' work.

And like Chigi's ostentatious ruse, it is also not without its sense of the illusory. Peruzzi's painted Hall of Perspectives in the Villa Farnesina may represent the highest order of architectural expression, but 'fantasy-artifice', in a world where 'form follows function' is now the default position, can easily sit ill with the architect. Archer Humphryes, however, feels that the creation of crafted illusion is not only desirable, but an implicit component of gastronomy. The firm cut its teeth in London on Hakkasan which, 12 years after it first opened, remains the best example of the highly curated gastronomic experience. But it was by no means the first. Archer Humphryes attributes the development of this culinary/ spatial metier to ten years earlier with Terence Conran's Quaglino's, Alan Yau's Wagamama and Oliver Peyton's Atlantic Bar and Grill in Piccadilly. It was Peyton who said "Restaurants should be about having fun"[x] and the Atlantic embodied the whole notion; part restaurant, part bar, part nightclub—a place not only to eat but to see and be seen—the whole dining event designed to meticulous levels of detail—the food part of a much broader sensory experience. By comparison, the likes of Le Gavroche, Langhams and The Ivy seemed stuffy and reactionary, their provenance from the old world of the Gentleman's Club brought suddenly into stark relief.

With Hakkasan, Archer claims, the visitor is complicit with the experience well before he even enters the restaurant's dark cavern-like depths. It was Yau's decision to site the restaurant in Hanway Place which, despite the regeneration of the Tottenham Court Road area, retains a sense of its being a dingy alley. Archer recounts the story of compiling a photographic 'gallery of horrors' of the street when they put in the application to Westminster planners. Yet it is precisely the counter-pointing of the move from a dowdy, sleazy street that makes the gradual descent into the hidden, dark, sultry, narcotic chinoiserie of Hakkasan so exciting. It is an experience that has been replicated and enhanced in Soho Mexican eatery La Bodega Negra, which requires the customer to negotiate the transgressive flashing neon of a sex shop in order to get to it.

Archer Humphryes took the same raw neon though in a less overt, more sophisticated and imaginative way in its Naamyaa (p 216) restaurant for Alan Yau, set within AHMM's Angel Building, and at Busaba Eathai (p 228) at Bicester Designer Village. The firm claims that creating the Asian experience for a restaurant totally decontextualised from the building in which it sits was a challenge but that, for inspiration, they were guided not by the cuisine, but by the idea of the creation of a sense of place; a distillation of the city of Bangkok. The inspiration, from visits to Bangkok drinking in the sights and sounds—was not those on the surface, but the sensations and drivers behind them. You will not find the obvious dark teak or Thai silks here; instead references are more oblique: Naamyaa is a blaze of neon, dominated by supergraphics, festooned by a wall of beaming buddhas. The vibrancy of the street life is here encapsulated—the adjacencies of food stalls with temples, tuk-tuks, market stalls and the ever-present sex industry. All of that chaos here surrounds Naamyaa's *raison d'être*—the kitchen itself—a sensory overload of wok flames and clashing steel—a heady cocktail of images, sounds and smells conjuring up the genius loci of Bangkok's frenetic city life.

Since creating the first Busaba eatery, the firm has done nine more and, perhaps counter to the idea of the creation of a franchise, is happy to go back to the drawing board and reformulate the design every time. In a sense this makes each a labour of love, born of the specificity of the particular conditions. Such thinking also resulted in the lofty offering at Bicester Designer Village which, contrary to the general approach by the retailers to hang suspended ceilings in the sheds, rose to fill the full height of the unit. Enter here, and you are immediately drawn into a gorgeously crafted interpretation of a traditional Thai Long House. And if Mercury-Prize winning rapper Ms Dynamite is to be believed, it is a place that is evocative enough to want to linger—she has gone to press saying that Busaba's the place she would most like to be locked into overnight.

Despite the practice's success in creating a cultural tableau within a dumb modernist box, one gets the sense that Archer Humphryes is more at home when extant conditions allow the architects to really draw on the site for inspiration, claiming that, for their Print Works restaurant, a basement in a 1930s Modernist building and past home of the *Bournemouth Daily Echo* newspaper, the design responded to its own logic. The old print room had high floor-to-ceiling heights, only high-level windows and a stark industrial aesthetic. The firm addressed each of these challenges in turn. The windows were fetishised by being framed in orange neon, the Modernist aesthetic boldly juxtaposed against the opulence of traditional crystal chandeliers; low-level suspended candle lamps above seating booths created intimacy in a space formerly devoid of any.

To a greater extent, the influence of the past makes itself palpably felt in the recent refurbishment of London's Great Northern Hotel (p 76) at King's Cross, where a rich history of terminus architecture was available for the firm to draw on. Here the sense of authenticity becomes more blurred—with many historical precedents of the typology already playing upon some notion of a fictional reality. Archer is quick to remark that the task was a lot easier at the St Pancras refurbishment where the narrative of Giles Gilbert Scott's hotel and Barlow's vast train shed behind it merely needed to be peeled away and re-revealed. At the Great Northern, without the legacy, the fantasy needed to be manufactured—with the firm claiming that its Houdini-like illusion of smoke and mirrors, pewter and leather in fact has, in common with past precedents, an illustrious genealogy. As at Paris' Gare de Lyon, the 1901 Le Train Bleu restaurant was in fact an ornately decorated Belle Époque fantasy inserted into an otherwise high-tech steel industrial shed. To visitors, the illusion was that this re-creation of a Versailles hall was an 'authentic' experience—which over time is only more embedded; Archer claims that what was done there has parallels with what the practice are doing at King's Cross—the same level of 'belief' applied to both scenarios.

That suspension of disbelief is evident at the Great Northern, which plays on the thrills of the liminal, transient nature of the terminus, to create a space charged with sexy potential. But it is more than surface deep—the environments bear up to scrutiny. Look around you—all the walnut furniture, drawing from the historical well of constructed fantasy, has been created bespoke for the spaces—all with subtle, contemporary turns. Such well-honed design follows in the wake of the great early Modernists such as Adolf Loos and Josef Frank, whose aim was to create rich, complete architectural interiors. Here, the furniture changes according to its position and use, be it in the bar, communal areas or in the formal dining room. The heady illusion is only convincing because it is both layered and nuanced—and ultimately because, with every room being treated as a one-off design process, the trick is never being repeated.

Both gastronomy and architecture deal with measurement, be it teaspoons or millimetres and the illusion too must also be robust enough to survive shifts in scale. The best spaces for food are the ones that consider everything from the finest detail of the place setting to the overall setting of the dining experience itself. Archer Humphryes explain that, in this regard, one of London's most successful establishments has to be The Wolseley. The venue is a modern creation but an evocation of a turn of the century Viennese cafe, from cutlery and crockery to chandeliers. However, the design's genius is the fact that the banquettes of the restaurant face the main entrance; and that once through this, the visitor finding themselves framed beneath a huge proscenium. For just a moment before taking a seat, the customer becomes an actor on a stage and the restaurant the audience. This one pivotal spatial move piques the vanity of the new guest, the curiosity of fellow diners and generates a dramatic tension rarely seen—culinary design sublimated into the realm of the theatrical.

Archer Humphryes would claim to be searching for this same alchemy. Certainly with the practice's more complex proposals for hospitality spaces, similar dramatic techniques are being employed. With its unexecuted proposal for the Croatian city of Split, the firm was faced with the challenge of a new-build luxury boutique hotel within spitting distance of the Roman ruins of Diocletian's Villa. Its response was to firstly incorporate elements of Roman planning into the new building—a great limestone square formed of long, thin Roman bricks, all the suites accessed off a central atrium space, obviating the need for corridors and creating a double aspect to all the rooms. To this the firm added another layer of reference that gave it further resonance with its context. Architect Robert Adam, who helped develop the eighteenth-century English Classical style, had visited the palace and drawn the Spalatro ruins in 1764; and in the firm's proposal, Adam revisits. Here rooms are adorned with giant baths, lights, mirrors and furniture—Adam details blown up to Brobdingnagian proportions.

their restraint and finesse suddenly decadent and indulgent, as the new context demands. Style is modern and abstracted, but based on ancient precedents as Adam's original sketches were but now imbued with the psychogeography of the place.

References to ancient Rome are evident again in the 63-room Sans Souci luxury hotel (p 106), set within a grand nineteenth-century block, just off Vienna's Ringstrasse. And here again, every bit of the building has been considered, examined and interrogated. Here, Loos-like reductivism is juxtaposed against outrageous Rococo decoration to create spatial polarities. The restaurant has a material restraint, following Le Corbusier's view that furniture should not overwhelm the art—a perfect environment for the client to show off their collection of twentieth-century masters whilst, in the bar, antique and Carlo Mollino furniture set within its gaudily gilded walls sets a seductive tone for the space. Archer Humphryes claim that, within its racy opulence, clients are invited to "behave badly", to relax, to let down their guards; to be exhibitionists or voyeurs—its cocktail-fuelled trysts a measure of the bar's intimacy; where even sleaze has a spatial place. And classical references abound—yet the moves being made are subtle reinterpretations carried out with rigour—a dialogue with the existing fabric of the building that is distinct from scholarly reproduction or pastiche. On the way into Sans Souci, a 20-metre long gallery of marble mosaic is lined with statues of classical muses, all leading to the hotel's lobby—a top-lit miniature of the Pantheon's coffered dome.

Re-used here, the form is a palimpsest of the original. But what in fact, is 'original'? The Pantheon's very existence can be put down to the fact that the nature of authenticity can change over time—it is likely that, had the building remained a Roman ruin, its stones would have been vandalised or stolen long before Boullée has the opportunity to use the form in his visionary homage to Newton, the 150-metre high Cenotaph. And it would never have been the dramatic backdrop for Peter Greenaway's fictional Kracklite for his slap-up homage to Boullée.

Greenaway's mise-en-scene is perfectly considered—not only making the obvious connection of the architect with the French visionary, but the more esoteric point that gastronomic pleasure involves the intellect. Here, as anywhere, a good meal piques the imagination, conjures memories and ideas, and the erudite, talented yet tortured Kracklite is a cipher for this. Where food and architecture come together, a kind of performative space is generated. And as the body tastes food, via the involvement of all the other sense—sight, sound, touch and smell—it is also intellectualising it, linking the meal with the context in which it is consumed.

What this raises is the convergence of taste as a sensory experience and taste as an aesthetic faculty, in a world where somehow they have become separated. The late architectural theoretician Marco Frascari noted that in Western culture the senses of sight and hearing have been given predominance, bemoaning how taste has been relegated to the lowest sense of all. However, he draws attention to the fact that, in its ancient understanding in Latin and Greek, 'taste' is a term that relates etymologically to the act of generating knowledge; that *sapienza* (wisdom) is related to *sapor*, taste. This reading of 'immediacy of understanding' has over time been corrupted to mean something impulsive—sensibility without reason.

Archer Humphryes' investigation into the architecture of entertainment and gastronomy, far from being a 'bums on seats, get-them-in, get-them-out' mentality, is in fact something far more sophisticated. It not only addresses the nature of the cuisine, but the context in which it is placed and, beyond that, draws on the psychogeography of the place itself. To underplay these themes is to not be cognisant of the key things that make great places great. Harry's Bar in Venice and Loos' American Bar in Vienna remain classic because they were designed to manifest hedonism and indulgence, and time has proved them to be timeless. This drive to understand the unique variables that will create dynamic and convivial spaces underpins everything that Archer Humphryes Architects does. Like the great French chef Antonin Carême, the son of an impoverished stonemason and architect of his famous *pièces montées*, his crafted table ornaments, the architects know that food and the spaces prepared for its consumption, must sublimate both senses of taste into one delicious idea.

THE CIVIC AND THE CITY
RE-OPENING MUNICIPAL MONUMENTS
EDWIN HEATHCOTE

There is a seriousness about London's nineteenth-century civic architecture. The Victorians and the Edwardians built their cities to last. There seemed to be an assumption at the time that this was a golden age, a confluence of the civic ambition of Medieval Gothic and the confident, educated hauteur of the Classical. They built solid buildings that had to resist not only the pollution in the air and the dirty pressure of the rookeries that often surrounded them but the turmoil and churn of a ground that was being dug up and displaced as tube lines and sewers were laid beneath them and the city was altered as it had never been before—and as it would never be since. This was an era of extraordinary change and invention, the canals and the railways sliced through the city, entire suburbs emerged in a few short years, streets were smashed through ramshackle lanes and alleys of Medieval timber. Electricity arrived along with the internal combustion engine, telegrams and telephones; the city became connected with the world.

The Victorians and the Edwardians built their buildings to anchor a city of incessant change, and also to become beacons in the fug of smog, mud, horse manure and construction dust, sturdy municipal monuments attesting to an idea of self and civic improvement. As the city grew, new building typologies emerged and architects sought expression in an eclectic cocktail which embraced Mannerism, Gothic, Queen Anne, flat-faced Georgian, vernacular and stolid urban Classicism. What should a hotel look like? A fire station? A library? A city school? There were no precedents, so the architects of late nineteenth- and early twentieth-century London applied themselves to creating new hybrid languages, curious, inventive mongrels of French Beaux Arts, Flemish town halls, country towns, guildhalls, villas, cathedrals and opera houses.

The results of this explosive era of architectural cross-breeding and the evolution of an English civic free-style have survived extraordinarily well. Despite the distaste of a generation of modernists who cared little for them and the insistent re-imaginations of the city around them, they remain moments of rigour and reliability in a contemporary cityscape which never seems to quite stand up against the confident, didactic, slightly arrogant brick and terracotta of its forebears.

So well have they survived, in fact, that they are often entering into their second, or even third incarnations, buildings too good to lose, with too much character and history engrained in their fabric to be replaced by anodyne contemporary buildings intended to last only a couple of decades. Archer Humphryes Architects' revivification of a trio of exactly these kinds of London buildings is an exemplar of respect for the quality of architecture and craftsmanship these buildings embody and the kind of ingenious adaptive reuse which ensures their futures.

The buildings here are a fire station, a railway hotel and a school. The perfect nineteenth-century blend of education, infrastructure and civic duty. That each is now becoming a hotel (in one case, being resurrected as a hotel) presents an intriguing picture of London in the twenty-first century. Each of these buildings was in a slightly neglected place, marginal zones on the cusp between wealth and poverty—or at least neglect. Not necessarily bad, not bad at all, but just slightly off the radar. The first, the Great Northern Hotel (p 76), stood between the rail behemoths of King's Cross and St Pancras stations; it could hardly have been more central yet it was a liminal, underused structure, its very form undermined by the changes wrought around it almost as soon as it was built. The second, the Manchester Square Fire Station in Chiltern Street, now Chiltern Firehouse (p 28), occupies a seemingly fine position in London's Marylebone but its fine Gothic features had faded into the urban background as it mouldered unused. The final building, the imposing St Olave's Grammar School in Southwark, now the Lalit Hotel London (p 292), is the kind of grand Edwardian Mannerist building which, despite its scale, has become part of the backdrop rather than the foreground of the city.

The earliest of the buildings is the Great Northern Hotel. Built in 1854 by the architect of the wonderful King's Cross station itself, Lewis Cubitt (1799–1883), it was to be the first of the great railway hotels. But less than two decades after it opened it was dwarfed by the neighbouring fairy tale-Gothic hulk of the Midland Grand Hotel in front of St Pancras Station. Its appearance also negated the curve in the road that had lent the Great Northern its distinctive form, rendering its elegant form curiously pointless. For the following century the building was abused and threatened, as schemes by Foster + Partners and John McAslan both proposed its demolition. Finally it was not only saved but its curving form became the generator of McAslan's new glass roofed concourse for King's Cross. The opening of the hotel betokened a moment in an incredible revival both of the station and its architect. The station has now become visible more-or-less as intended—without the detritus of forecourts and shops which destroyed the public space outside it for decades—and the ensemble of hotel and station has been joined by another Cubitt building, the nearby vast, one-time granary which has been revivified as the new Central Saint Martins art school. Suddenly all three of these buildings by a key architect of London's landscape have been revived as real public spaces, accessible and useful, like reappearances on a Nolli plan of an area that was once characterised by dumb inaccessibility, the leftover infrastructural no-man's-land of the post-industrial city.

The revival of the hotel has been characterised by its reintegration into the expanded architectural landscape surrounding the station. The most marked change has been the carving into the ground floor of an arcade which, whilst counterintuitive in the loss of valuable lobby and bar space, has had the effect of opening the building out, making it feel public, as much a part of the concourse as the city—an urbanity amplified by the addition of an all-hours fresh food kiosk built in to the wall serving both city and station. The bar consequently has the hybrid buzz of a grand station and a downtown destination, a feel amplified by the highly polished zinc bar (which curves in an echo of the building itself), the mirrored ceiling, marble, chequerboard floor and rich Venetian chandeliers. Even if it is not large, it has the urban ambition of a grand nineteenth-century room and it concentrates the activity of the now Janus-faced building into a tight, dynamic space that is both intimate and dynamic. Upstairs the Plum & Spilt Milk restaurant is more expansive, darker and less jazzy, centred around a suspended constellation of smoky hand-blown glass lampshades. The bespoke furniture creates an undulating landscape of warm, highly polished hardwood and soft green leather which evokes something of the round-the-clock urbane comfort of a Viennese coffee house. The rooms look onto the cityscape, station and towers, a gritty glimpse of a London which changes yet somehow remains resolutely recognisable. Specially-designed furniture sparkles with a hint of the one-time glamour of travel, its blend of polished metal, rich wood and streamlined corners evoking the trunks and stands of portable living —in an age of porters.

Towards the west of the city, near another of London's great terminals, Marylebone, stood for years another seemingly unloved building. The old fire station in Chiltern Street was, however, a magical building of refined craftsmanship and an augur of an emerging building type that was to become a London speciality, the red-brick fire station. Built in 1889 the neo-Gothic-cum-Tudor building was an early effort in the London County Council's pioneering programme of purpose-built fire stations across the city in a recognisable, if always changeful, style. Designed by the chief architect of the Metropolitan Board of Works' fire station department, Robert Pearsall, the small building's history exemplifies the radical changes in technology over the short period bridging the turn of the century. What was once a station for horse-drawn engines carrying leather fire hoses with a fire-watchtower (which pokes above the parapet like something from Medieval Bruges or Ghent) and emergency bell for fire alerts was, within a couple of decades of completion, obliged to accommodate more or less modern tenders, telephones and electrics. Its charming cocktail of Flemish Gothic and proto-Arts and Crafts detail, delicate stonework and a nod to Norman Shaw's mansion blocks set the style for the future stations which evolved into some of the LCC's most characteristic buildings. But those same quirky details and its fine city-centre location also make for a well-placed small hotel. The scale of the appliance sheds on the ground floor gives the building its public areas— bars and restaurants which feel like urban spaces with arches that feel almost like arcades. The internal structure, with its stripped-down cast iron columns and riveted beams meanwhile evokes a particular kind of New York space, an intense, industrial, loft-ish room, a curious moment in an otherwise archetypally London landscape.

The courtyard meanwhile becomes an outside dining area, a rare space for release in a dense, tight-knit part of the city. The variegated, picturesque nature of a series of elevations has allowed the architects to skilfully slot in new elements which appear indistinguishable from the complex profile of the original—yet which are in fact significantly expanded, notably at the rear.

The grandest of all three buildings is the former Lambeth College, a hugely impressive Edwardian pile which manages to be somehow almost invisible from the traffic-clogged artery of Tower Bridge Road. Built as St Olave's Grammar School in 1893–1894, the building was the work of one of the most successful Edwardian architects, Edward Mountford (1855–1908). A prolific builder of libraries, colleges and town halls, Mountford's eclectic style typified the civic pomposity— but also the grand generosity—of Edwardian civic architecture. Best known as the architect of the New Sessions House at the Old Bailey, Mountford's 'Wrenaissance' designs blended the familiar elements of English Baroque with an urbane brick solidity. The scale of the South London college is almost breathtaking. From the lofty barrel-vaulted assembly hall to the decorated interiors of the headmaster's rooms with their grand fireplaces and intricately moulded ceilings, the grand spaces of a city hotel are already present, almost ready-made.

The interior designs envision a kind of Deco-cum-colonial grandeur. With a touch of Joseph Urban and a dash of Hollywood Persian, the aim is to make a sober civic building into an exotic public space. Whilst it is true that the latter two of these three buildings were once civic infrastructure and are being transferred to a private realm, it is equally true that a hotel is one of the pivotal public spaces of the city. Already at the Great Northern the vibrancy of the bars and restaurants has revived a certain glamour long lacking at the station and a permeability that has returned the interiors to the everyday life of the city. These latter two buildings, civic in name but actually long empty and impenetrable to the public even when they were functioning, also bring back beautiful works of well-crafted and carefully-considered municipal building into use and delight. These are buildings whose elevations, craftsmanship and sculptural form had always adorned the streetscape but which will soon open themselves up to the day-and-night cycle of city life.

CHILTERN FIREHOUSE

Built in 1887–1889 after the creation of London's first publicly funded brigade, Manchester Square Fire Station has been transformed into a remarkable hotel. The ladder shed is now the living room, the former fire officer's dormitories are now exquisite handcrafted suites, the appliance room is the restaurant made instantly famous on opening by a guest list that includes presidents and artists.

In 2010, Archer Humphryes Architects began the distinguished architecture for what was to become the Chiltern Firehouse recognised in recent architecture awards. As hotelier André Balazs' first property in Europe, the project demanded exceptional results from the architects, continuing a hotel portfolio that included the Chateau Marmont in Los Angeles and The Mercer in New York. A long-term friend and collaborator, he knew that the practice would carry out a truly impressive scheme. Leading the construction for André's impressive investors including Manhattan Loft Corporation, the Portman Estate and distinguished individuals—Google's Eric Schmidt (who was given a tour at the beginning when the building still consisted of the night-duty sleeping quarters of the nineteenth century)—was a tremendous commission for the architects.

Sweeping through the city of London in 1666, the Great Fire destroyed the Medieval street plan. 'Watchmen' and gunpowder explosions were organised by public-spirited citizens, along with the tower of every church holding long ladders and leather buckets—the precursor to a modern fire brigade. The fire station was originally built in masonry, an important material change replacing the former Medieval timber structures that had exacerbated former infernos. The fire station would once again be rooted within civic history, this time as a hotel. Initially planned with stables and watch posts, amongst other functions, the eccentric building follows on from the churches designed by Christopher Wren that, for two centuries, took the role of fire surveillance, from each building's look-out. Wren utilised Vitruvius' treatise from antiquity that asserts structure must exhibit virtues of *"firmitas, utilitas, venustas"*—that is, it must be "solid, useful, beautiful"—the only surviving ancient prescriptive architecture text.[2]

Architectural historian Andrew Saint described Robert Pearsall's original state organised building as the best surviving example of the Gothic style used by London fire stations, which he noted as being: "distinctive, arresting and original with their angular outline, paired windows, prickly detailing and crenelated look out towers".[3] Through scholastic enquiry into both the external and interior architecture, Archer Humphryes found inspiration in the form and details of the original building as they sought to blend its history with the requirements and expressions of the new use.

A pivotal architectural decision was the addition of a new independent wing stitched to the existing building and the reinstatement of the original Portland stone facade, Archer Humphryes deployed modern methodologies to resolve the exuberant Gothic style, bringing to the project the practice's extensive knowledge of stone detailing in the application of new ogee arches, carved rosettes, crenelated parapet, articulated gabled buttresses as well as the fluted columns that line the openings for the glazed concertina doors.

Proportion was integral to the new architecture from the start. Before creating the new five-storey tower joined seamlessly to the fully remodelled fire station, the practice studied Pearsall's original drawings in order to generate a design that retained the intrinsic character of the site's history. The result was a new facsimile 'sister' that sits alongside the original building. The *tour de force* of the new architecture however is a prominent new gable end facing Chiltern Street, complete with cathedral window containing carved stone trefoil motifs inset within the brickwork depth. The conservatory bar at the ground floor opens onto a discrete cobbled garden. Bricks are handmade to imperial dimensions to align with existing coursing, and bonded with precise, vertical joints.

Archer Humphryes worked closely with André Balazs' in-house design team and the designers Studio KO to design each of the 26 hotel suites to reflect the idea of domesticity, a home. Each suite is designed to reflect the personality of the hotel owner, at the same time optimising the available natural light and the particularities of the site, with different details adding a sense of enchantment for the guests.

Public areas of the hotel are ornamental, luxurious, full of texture and have been compared to "Palm Beach seen through a Hollywood glow". In the reception, dramatic straw panels with powerful single lines of interwoven colour create a strong abstract pattern. The walls of the conservatory bar are wrapped in honey hues of onyx, cradled below a ceiling of basket panels lined with gilded golden frames.

André Balazs' holistic approach to the curation of the hotel artwork is nineteenth-century in derivation, where every element of the interior's sensual experience contributes to the wellbeing and pleasure of the guests while they live or relax in the hotel. When a Dali painting appeared irreverently taped to the wall during a party, the hotel began its own narrative of heydays straight out of an Oscar Wilde novella. The result is a project that sits somewhere between 'museum,' and 'theatre'. As in Guy Debord's *La Société du Spectacle,* the idea is to "wake up the spectator who has been drugged by spectacular images... through radical action in the form of the construction of situations that bring a revolutionary reordering of life, politics, and art".[4] Today concepts still take their departure from Vitruvius' ancient theatre design where life exists in performance and congregation, except today perhaps the spectacle is found in secular surroundings of a regular restaurant in the profane surroundings of a hotel which was formerly a fire station.

STATION

New Tower Wing Building has prominence over the cobbled garden and bridges the infamous Ladder Shed, now the exclusive hotel's living room and the original fire station.

A restored cast iron quatrefoil and stone pediment revealing acanthus foliage illustrate the attention to detail in creating an exceptional architecture that has become a preeminent London destination.

FIRE · BRIGADE · STATION

Principal facade with reinstated Portland stone. Westminster Planning Department now promotes the project's architectural accomplishment as an example of exemplary planning in London.

A replica fire lantern hangs above the former Appliance Room, where Venetian stonework details are reintroduced along with the reinstatement of columns with pilasters and capitals on the echelon, all of which had been lost with the installation of concrete lintels and steel shutters in the 1960s.

Kent peg tiles with a fish scallop pattern are added to the Victorian arch reveal of the concertina timber doors that open up the Chiltern Firehouse to the street. Three carved ogee arches with rosettes frame restaurant doorways and organise the internal arrangement of the table settings.

Stone crenulations add a rhythm to the principal facade that separates the brickwork, whilst a carved quatrefoil with a central heraldic shield abuts the pediment buttress.

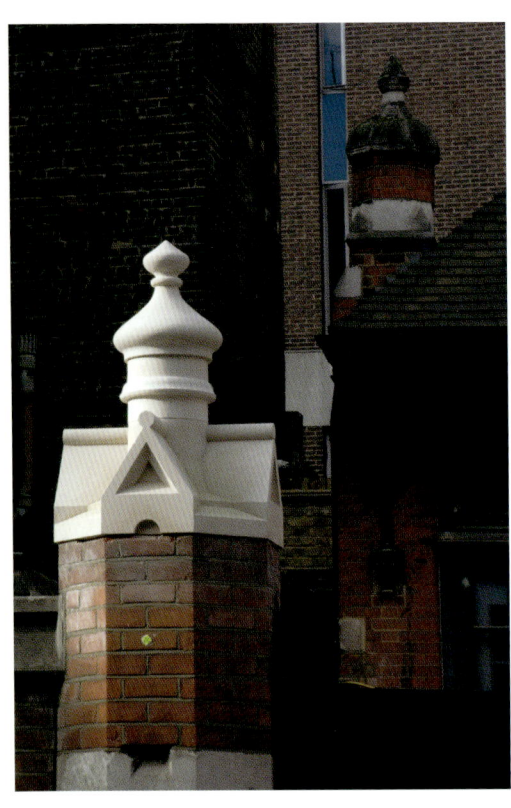

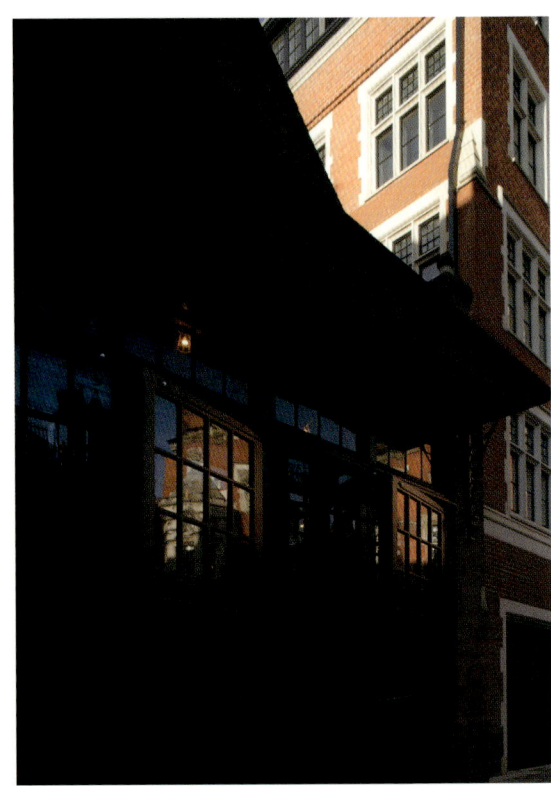

Handmade imperial Faversham red bricks matching the original Acton red bricks and a new crow step gable end with ogee carved copings.

A cathedral window crowns the new architecture, which sits perpendicular to the original facade. A restored Oriel window, set against the soaring fluted stacks, is a memory of the Gothic Revivalist architecture. What used to be the look-out for the station master's accommodation is now newly appointed as one of the 26 luxury quarters in the hotel.

An octagonal buttressed Watch Tower, which
formerly was used for hose drying and look-out for
fires before the telephone existed, punctuates the
skyline becoming an intimate belvedere for two,
commanding spectacular views of the city.

Sommelier's passage and the
cellar vaults below the street.

Nero Marquina and tumbled Rouge Verona floor tiles housed
within an industrial steel conservatory painted dissolute
black and containing exotic plants forms the entrance to the
hotel. Influenced by the architects' visits to Keble College
in Oxford which was designed by William Butterfield, a
contemporary of the fire station's original architect, Robert
Pearsall, the entrance resembles a European winter garden.

Here the architects have added steps to the kitchen to create a stage for the chefs, with the Bonnet range stoves in brass and black enamel from Lyon, dominating the room vistas in the former appliance room.

Rubbing magnetic noses of the salt and pepper tableware add humour; a mirror screen against a seating enclosure reflects the room endlessly—providing delineation in the table arrangements.

The firemen's pole is reset within a red half-moon booth whilst a woven Jute from India set between reclaimed timber joists with exposed Black Japonned nails in the ceiling above creates an unexpected solution to acoustic panelling, introducing primary colour and texture. Glazed Minton tiles were discovered after scraping decades of magnolia paint from the walls.

Selected timber furniture harmonises with
the nineteenth-century kitchen ambience the
architects have created with a quarry tile floor
surface, a marble counter top adjacent to the open
kitchen and utilitarian pantry black pendants.

Chef's table seating 12 with herbs set out on the window ledge continues the informal kitchen garden atmosphere.

Seating 120 people, each table is
arranged differently in the space
where the fire carriages once were.

Mahogany message and key boxes are panels to the reception wall. A straw woven ceiling from Paris laid out in a square grid pattern has an indigo thread stitching echoing simple furniture details in the interior, introduced to add texture and warmth.

Bedrooms entrances are adorned with Brigade Red, hand brushed gloss paint with a patinated scratch plate and cast brass door knob manufactured by Ize with dressed screws, window seats in the sleeping area evoke Voyseys' Windermere Arts and Crafts materials, brass golden mesh backlit is used in wardrobe furniture and Bakelite switch plates add homage to the original use of the firemen's quarters.

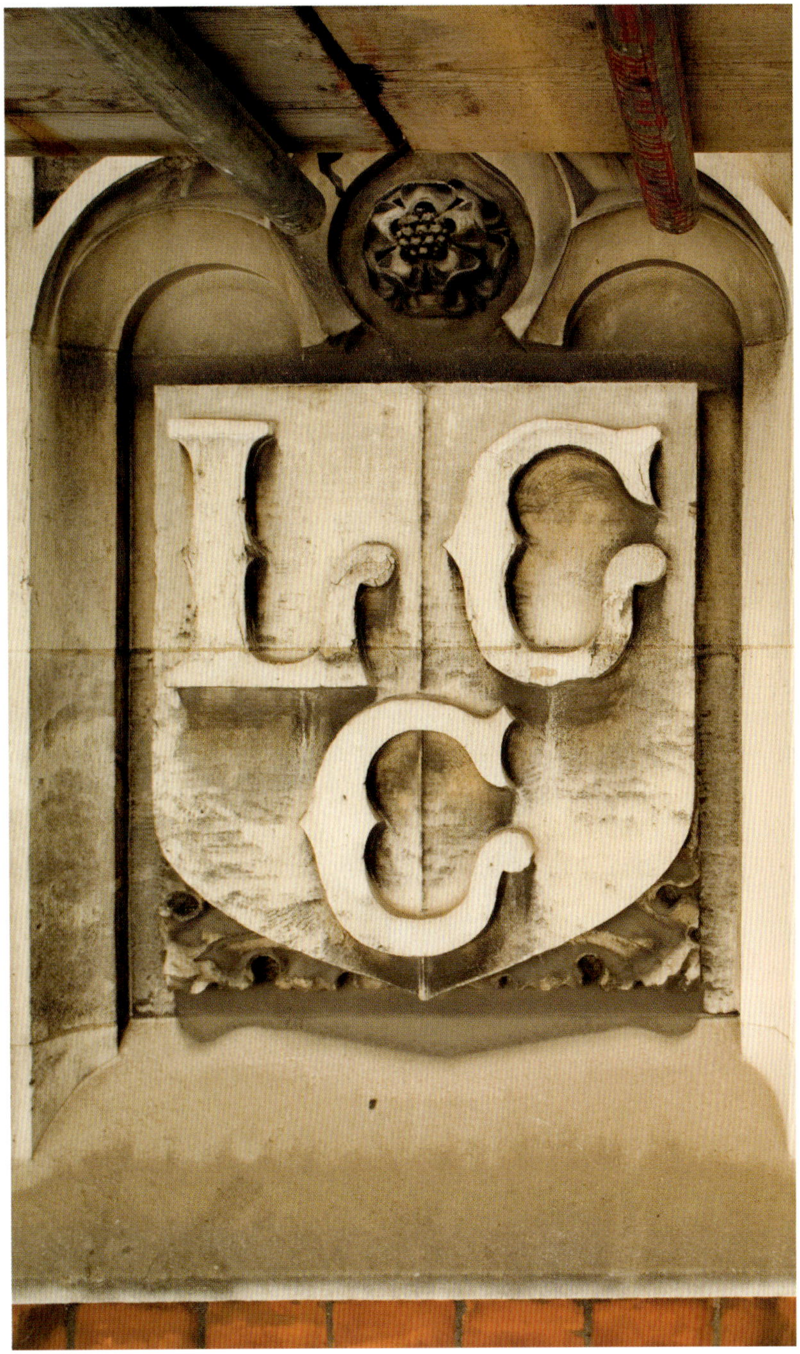
LCC

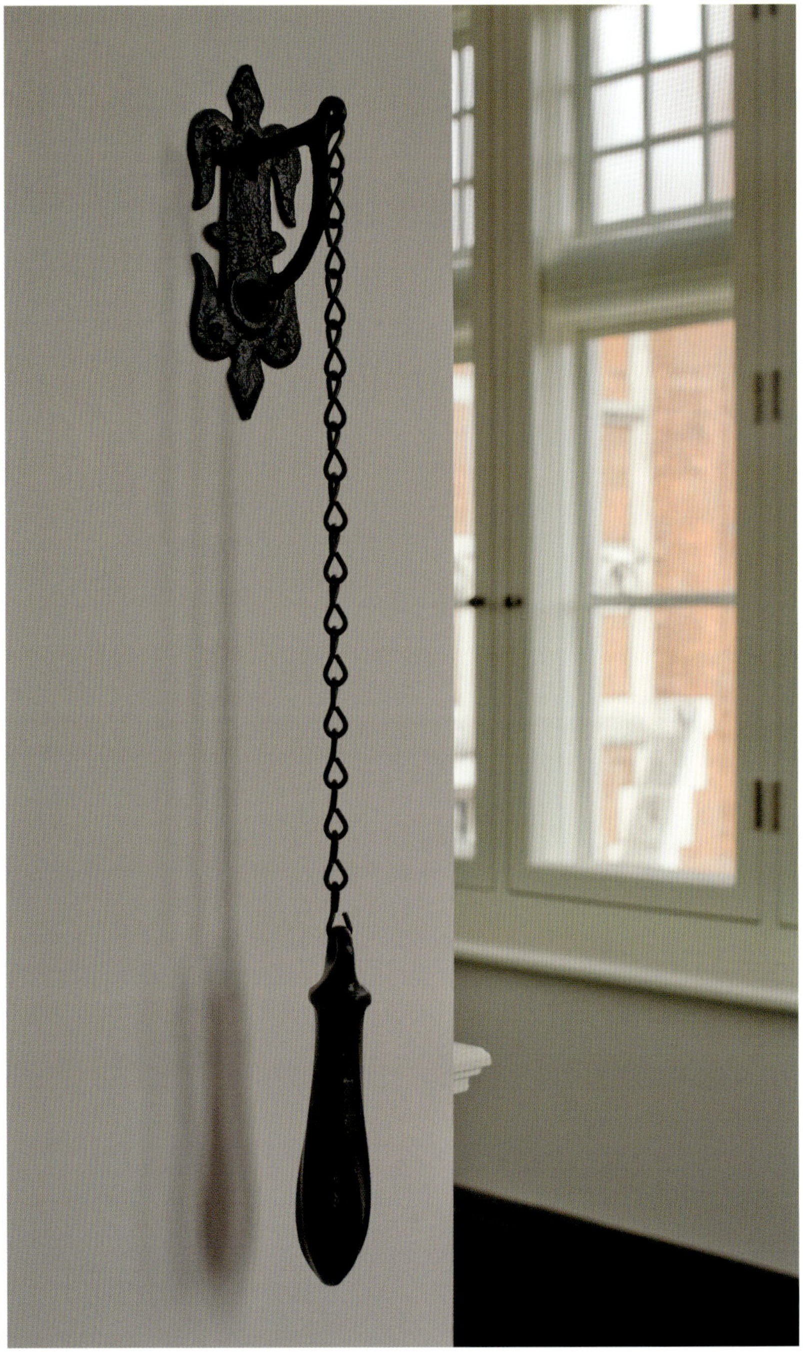

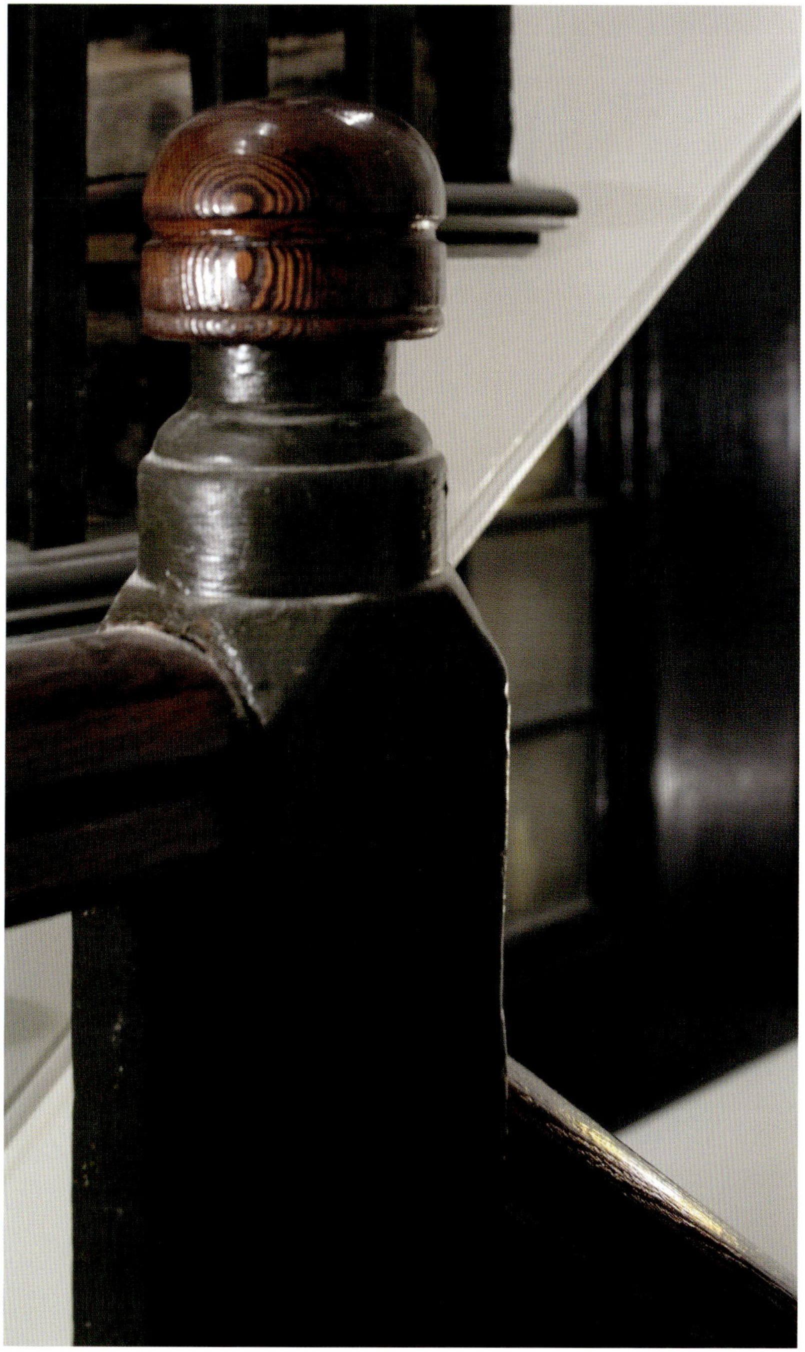

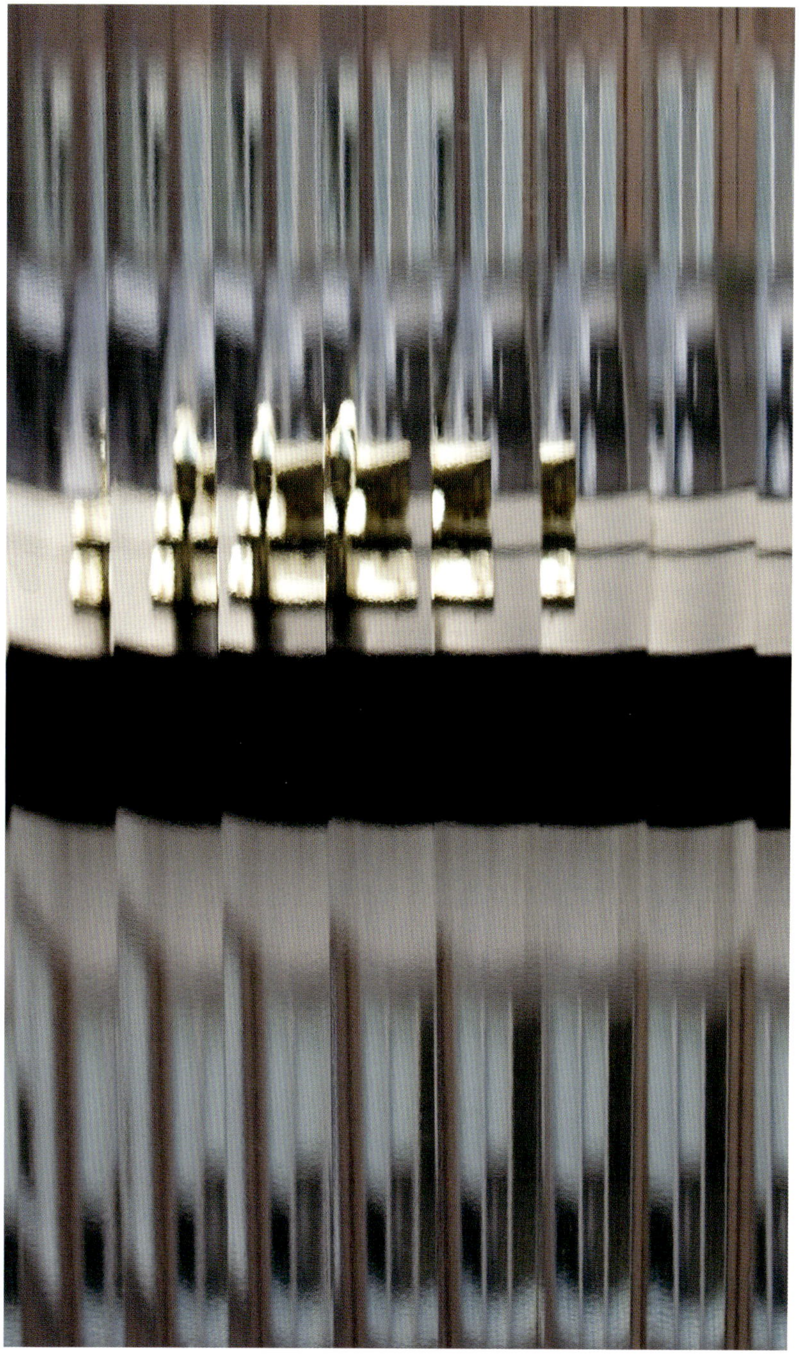

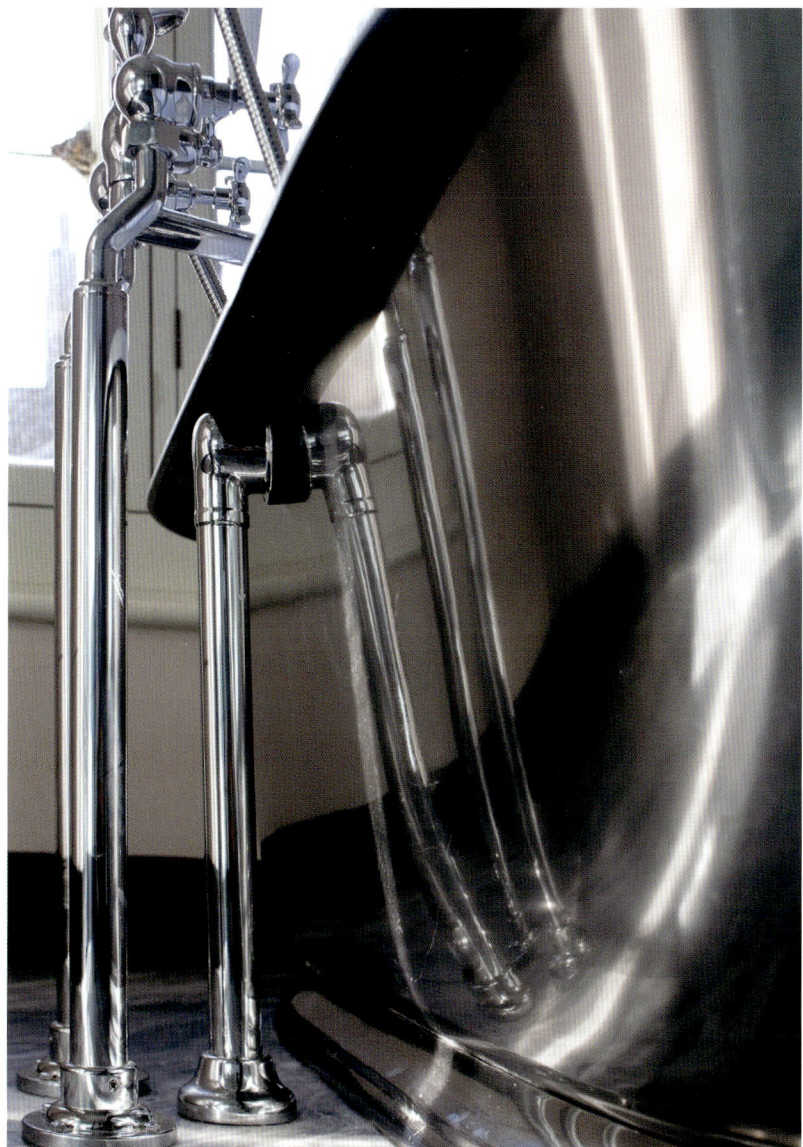

The silver Tamar double-ended bath in polished cast iron reveals natural pitting as a leitmotif of the handmade quality of the bathing areas, with natural light reflecting the nuances of the London lighting against surround blush pink gloss walls.

Cornecia Grigio selected for its marble graphic quality and applied as slab flooring, accents the hand-thrown glazed sea green tiles; their luminosity splits the spectrum between blue and green, with reflections in the room.

Stripped walls revealed Arsenic Green coloured paint with a primary red plimsoll line—the original nineteenth-century firemen's colour scheme. Kept as discovered, the main walls in the Ladder Shed are without further adornment, painstakingly stripped back using a toothbrush.

Stairway to the Watch Tower where the original ventilation shaft provided fresh air to the stables for the horses that pulled the engine carriages. Now it is the ascent to the intimate Belvedere look-out.

GREAT NORTHERN HOTEL

Myth has it that a major battle took place between the Romans and Boudicca, the warrior queen of the Iceni, on the site of King's Cross where the Great Northern Hotel is sited. Urban folklore even suggests that Boudicca is buried beneath platforms 9 and 10 next to the hotel. Whatever the truth, both King's Cross and Boudicca—whose name derives from the Celtic for victory—enjoyed something of a revival in the Victorian era. Development of the area, fuelled by the building of King's Cross station, took on epic proportions. Meanwhile Queen Victoria became equated with her namesake Boudicca, whose fame subsequently grew anew.

When Lewis Cubitt's creation, The Great Northern Hotel, opened in 1854, it was the world's first railway terminus hotel. This transport hub status was to become a perpetual symbol for Archer Humphryes when owner Jeremy Robson gave the practice the titanic task of recovering, rebuilding and transforming the building back to its former glory after years of neglect.

At a time when the surrounding area was undergoing rapid regeneration, engaging with its urban context as the gateway to King's Cross was a recurrent 'absolute' for the architects. They also took inspiration from the *Belle Époque* era, a time of romantic railway glamour. Lady Violet, a famous resident of the time, became a heroine for the project, lending her name to the bar's signature cocktail.

When guests step over the threshold of the hotel from the busy metropolis, it is imperative to the architects that they should find themselves in an intimate interior that captures the surrounding vibrancy of the city but at the same time is a sanctuary from the busiest transport intersection in Europe. The challenge was how to reconcile in the project's design these apparent opposites of openness and protection.

A comforting hotel reception and a vibrant GNH bar at the ground floor connect the revamped King's Cross Station and Eurostar terminal in St Pancras. The dominant colours in the bar are black, red, chocolate and silver. The black of the Italian marble bar follows the curvaceous crescent form of the buildings with more black marble on the floor, and black Cordoba leather trimming and stitching to the blinds. Red velvet drapery enveloping the entrances combines with walnut panelling, a reference to the original teak fittings of vintage passenger locomotives. There are flashes of silver everywhere, in the pewter on the bar surface and in

the reflective mirrored ceiling that accentuates the dazzling brilliance of the crystal chandeliers so reminiscent of *Belle Époque* interiors. The bar's romantic character is completed by the furniture pieces which have been designed by the architects to provide guests with respite and drama. For some critics the design is evocative of other historical station bars such as the Oyster Bar at Grand Central Station in New York and Le Train Bleu at Gare de Lyon in Paris.

The Plum & Spilt Milk restaurant is on the upper floor, taking its name from the distinctive dining livery of the Flying Scotsman that first pulled into King's Cross with Queen Victoria aboard in 1851. Symmetrically ordered, the theatrical space benefits from breathtaking views of George Gilbert Scott's iconic clock tower at St Pancras and the new piazza. By day, the dining room is bathed in delicious coolness generated by sunlight flooding in from several directions. By night, 150 hand blown transparent glass lanterns create a chimerical amber quality. A reference to historic enamelled railway signage, Hague Blue was selected as a characterful backdrop to the ensemble and to accentuate the black, cracked lava tables from Mount Etna and curved leather banquettes, all designed by the architects.

Upstairs, there are 91 hotel rooms sitting within the building's original cross-wall construction. Curved corridors, designed originally to suit the crinoline dresses of the time, run the length of the building and inform the proportions of the new spaces. There are three room types. The Couchette is intended to evoke the classic continental railway sleeper car, which the architects had experienced travelling from Moscow to St Petersburg on the infamous night train Krasnaya Strela. Wainscot rooms are ravishingly swathed in American walnut panelling and a deep 'plum' palette, while Cubitt rooms have been described as "timeless elegance and grace with a twist of modernity and a touch of sensuality".[5] Every last detail is chosen or designed by the architects, from the travel embroidery case on the bedside table to the herringbone slate and porcelain tiles of the bathroom.

It has been a challenging five-year journey, fuelled by the imagination of the architects and also the client's determination to create a place of both "beatitude" and "*élan vital*" in the city. But finally, and triumphantly, the Great Northern Hotel has arrived back at its original destination as one of the finest luxury hotels in the capital, just as it was when it first opened in 1854.

The West Crescent now adjoined to King's Cross' Western Concourse has 58 million passengers passing annually through the hotel's arcade. The dormer slate roof extension is visible, with Gilbert Scott's St Pancras clock tower looming in the background.

The south elevation of the hotel, which faces King's Cross Square with the original 1854 stock brick Italianate, has been transformed, creating a more considered relationship between the hotel and its surroundings for the first time since it was built. Being saved from the 1987 masterplan which proposed demolishing the Grade II listed building to be replaced by the Eurostar Terminal, it took seven years' dedication to bring the derelict building back to life.

At dusk the bar interior radiates, with Parisian style awnings marking the entry. A train termini hot spot reminiscent of grand old stations was the influence where, as *Observer* columnist Jay Rayner observed, "at midnight the cafe was always full of travellers changing trains and the espresso machines steamed constantly as if in tribute to the old puffers that once passed by".

Here in the bar, the architects have introduced a pewter bar top with traditional chandeliers which reflect vibrantly throughout the room in the Venetian mirrored ceiling.

Nero Marquina marble forms a solid curved base to the bar, anchored to a chequered marble floor.

Bohemian glassmakers from the
Czech Republic, known for the
purity of their crystal, made the
chandeliers to the architects' design.

The bar is an island in composition
in planning layout, allowing the
spectacular proportion of the windows
to be admired without interruption to
the perimeter of the room.

The architects have designed simple and contemporary
circular tables with radial patterns, complementing
high-back, elliptical, walnut banquettes. The ensemble
of cream leather and high gloss lacquer was deliberately
chosen to evoke the enduring feeling of bygone *Belle
Époque* and nineteenth-century zinc bars' cafe furniture.

A lounge reminiscent of a luxury vintage carriage travelling across Continental Europe, with a curved walnut ceiling in linear boards, is the waiting area for the restrooms.

A 'snug' in the bar allows for some visual respite from the main bar area, with its mirrored ceiling. A cafe chair in solid walnut striated will not look out of place in 50.

In the centre, traversing the building on each floor, is a naturally-lit corridor with the Victorian sash windows restored. Its width was generated by Victorian ladies' fashion etiquette—two women should be able to pass in the corridor without embarrassment, despite the breadth of their petticoats. Room numbering in simple enamelled plates inspired by the original GNH carriage livery identity, and curved carpet runners, create quietude in a building located on one of the busiest intersections in London.

Grand stair restored; its position directly impacted upon the arrangement of the principal rooms. 'Lulworth Blue' picks up the metal work on the balustrade with the handrail retaining its simple elongation. The same blue is used in Gilbert Scott's Gothic Revival metal structure in the adjacent property of St Pancras.

A buttoned sofa in French Grey
leather is close to a pantry where
guests can find coffee and take the
opportunity to meet and exchange
stories with other travellers.

Here in the Cubitt Room, the height
provides serenity and the room is calm.
Olive Green paintwork absorbs the
light and enhances the simple white
porcelain pendant and silver signal
lamps beside the bed.

Selected for their timeless qualities, white irregular glazed tiles glimmer against the porcelain basin.

Dark Cumbrian slate set in a herringbone pattern on the floor, the bright white of the bath and the mirror's proportion assist in absorbing natural daylight onto the walls of the bathing area.

Showers capture sunlight from the outside, through fluted glass doors for the discretion of the occupants.

Next to the bed the architects placed a *bauletto* table. Choosing chrome and curved walnut, they designed the table and the decorative mirrors to accentuate the industrial age of the property, exemplified by the 'Signal Lamp' at the bedside. *Bauletto* is the Italian word for the travel vanity cases that used to be carried on the Orient Express to Venice.

From the sofa, which was designed by the architects to be lightweight with a solid curved walnut back, the powerful ascending clock tower frames the vista on entry. Added touches of a self-adjusting pendant, in porcelain, above an occasional table for eating or working, add to the versatility for the guest who can make adjustments according to their own desires.

Named by the architects, the Couchette room is evocative of a luxury sleeping compartment; the walls are painted in London Clay paint, while the bed is set against the window, poised above the glass station concourse canopy.

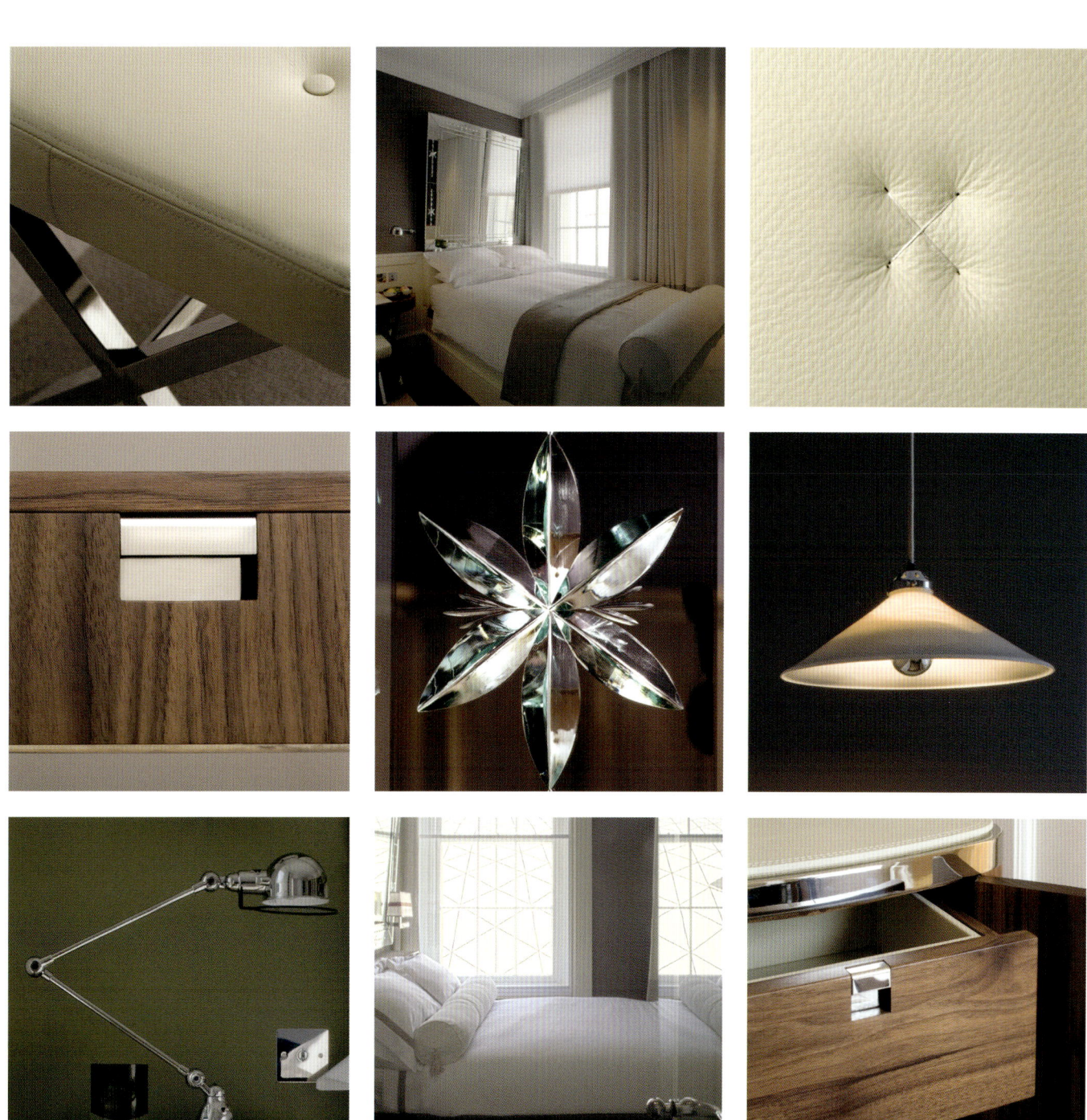

Silver metallic surfaces for mirrors, furniture
tops and flush clutch handles in chrome, glass,
stainless steel and pewter; sumptuous cream
leather continues into linings of the furniture;
Venetian cut-glass motifs and Italian linens
add a twist of elegance.

The Plum & Spilt Milk restaurant romantically reinstates the romance of a Grand Railway Hotel dining room, occupying the first floor, and with panoramic views in all directions. Working ingeniously with the structure, the architects succeeded in adding this room to the public spaces of the hotel; in the new masterplan of King's Cross —which the client inherited in the scheme—the former opulent ground floor public rooms had dramatically been absorbed into the footprint of the station, lost from the hotel forever.

Cream and tan leather banquettes winding around the room, walnut panels with traditional Dimity White eggshell for window architraves and shutters and a modern herringbone patterned floor witness the changing day and light scenes in this theatrical interior.

After mixing colours to create the exacting tone for the first glass shade, in a furnace reaching a 1,000 degrees, brushed brass was selected for the lamp holder and a twisted golden cord was found. The finishing touch was the selection of the nostalgic incandescent tungsten filament dipped in antique silver reminiscent of street gas lanterns from the era of the building's construction.

Black lava stone from Mount Etna forms the table surface and is edged with brushed satin brass to match the lanterns. Tableware mirrors the metallic brass with napkin holders and plate edgings. An occasional plum appears graphically on the cream plates taken from the distinctive livery of the dining cars of the Flying Scotsman that pulled out of King's Cross in Queen Victoria's reign.

In this room, the architects have created simple, contemporary furniture, which concentrates the focus upon hundreds of chromatic hand blown amber gold glass lanterns.

(top left) A fluted glass wall, internally illuminated, provides a spectacular filmic sequence to the bar with the stools outlined in silhouette when the lights dim into the late evening.

Movement is visually arresting within the restaurant, the arrangement is indicative of the architectural language for the entire hotel: defining the key rational order of the space before populating with loose fittings, furniture and accessories, creating and imaginative environment to participate in.

(top right) The fluted glass in the building's design is continued in the glassware itself, echoing the architecture, with red cut glass candleholders reflected in the black and gold marble table surface.

Hague Blue, originally a Dutch external woodwork paint, deadens light, making it a suitable colour for a picture gallery where focal lights showcase the art collection of the owner.

Brass satin edges to black and gold marble table tops follow the proportions of the chair arm's solid walnut. Light floods into the room and reflects on the brass accents and lacquered timber.

SANS SOUCI HOTEL VIENNA

Located within the bohemian museum quarter known most famously for Klimt's *The Kiss* that hangs in the Belvedere Palace, Sans Souci Hotel Vienna is in the heart of the most cultural city of music in Europe.

On being commissioned to create the architecture and interiors for Norbert Winkelmayer, the architects quickly took his passion and cue to create an independent hotel that would showcase his impressive collection of contemporary art.

With a complex task ahead of them—with so many cultural references to select from—Archer Humphryes began the substantial challenge: a complete review of what the preceding Viennese team had achieved and what the ambition for the project would be. This seemingly impossible activity was made more difficult still by the fact that renovation work had already commenced on site and the design would have to adapt to certain decisions already taken.

How then to combine the grandiose spaces with an inviting intimate atmosphere, while simultaneously maintaining Archer Humphryes' original architectural language of elegance and restraint? Analysing the content, responding to the ethical humanistic context, reduction of the disparate rooms, organisation of the private and public realm of the hotel and not presupposing whom the community of the hotel 'should be' is how the project was approached. Creating the canvas for a public building in the broader, more radical definition by 'not belonging to anyone'—ultimately meaning that, when a guest arrives, he or she 'possesses' the space; the design's role is to await their arrival to claim ownership. Under the rubric of 'ornamentation', the visual distinction between organisation of architecture, structure and participation of the visitor are not separated; they are part of the same creation.

A distinguished history, with an aristocratic quality in the noble sense of Vienna's former grand hotels was the architects' starting point. In the late nineteenth century, it operated as the Hotel Høller and before that had hosted the world premier of Johann Strauss' *Tritsch-Tratsch Polka* when it was an Inn. At the height of the Habsburg Austro-Hungarian Empire, in the capital Vienna, the polka, imported from Russian society, was a vibrant, energetic dance. Attachment to this spirit was to be combined with the client's personal art collection of Picassos, Kaufmans and Lichtensteins to grace the walls of the project.

Particular care was taken to ensure that the renovations of the exterior and interior preserved the character of the area, something Archer Humphryes truly respected in a city of many architectural treasures. In the interiors, guests approach the hotel via a rotunda reception, along a gallery, leading immediately into the hotel and bar. The visitor is then lead to the spa with its calm pool and then quietly to the peaceful bedrooms.

All of the spaces are a reminder of the hotel's location in the city's culture. As always, the furniture has been specifically crafted for the entire hotel, made to measure. Interspersed with antiques and referencing Norbert Winkelmayer's passion for design classics by including pieces by Mollino, Jacobsen and Cherner as well as Starck's iconic stools, Archer Humphryes painstakingly compiled the choices with the client, designing objects to complement the interior.

It is in the public areas where the design was able to showcase the tribute to the city's glorious past. The restaurant bar was inspired by the '*cabine glacé*' of eighteenth-century Viennese palaces. The carved panelled and mirrored walls provide the endless reflection of points of light from the carved gold chandeliers, with decadent velvet furnishings found in the classic palaces, where Franz Ferdinand was one of the last residents before the revolution and his assassination. An amber glow of gold in the finishes embodies the entwinement of the lovers in *The Kiss*. The influence of the opposites of both the linear constructs of the contemporary Art Nouveau style and the organic forms of the earlier Arts and Crafts Movement that *The Kiss* encapsulates became a constant reference point for the architects throughout their work. The restaurant complements the bar in vitality and changing scenes throughout the day. Floors are inlaid with sycamore marquetry reliefs that mirror Hapsburg interiors, seen as far away as Zagreb, and wall reliefs have fluted pilaster that comes from a long Viennese tradition of craftsmanship.

This decadence and opulence is what the client describes as a "charismatic luxury", contrasted with the hotel's namesake '*sans souci*'—'without concerns', symbolising the hotel as a place of relaxation rather than a seat of power. It is this aspect that has given Archer Humphryes the opportunity to make a strikingly modern, yet evocative hotel, securing its place as a leading European hotel shortly after opening.

Situated on Burggasse, the hotel holds an enviable location next to the Museum Quarter. A typical nineteenth century Habsburg city block, the building once housed the Zum Grossen Zeisig venue where Johann Strauss premiered his *Tritsch-Tratsch Polka* in 1858. Archer Humphryes returned the street facades to their original glory by reintroducing wooden window casements and balconies on the principal street elevations, along with new interventions such as the glass Winter Garden on Museumstrasse, a white stucco to the frontage and elliptical canopies in emperor purple.

In this gallery a sense of arrival is achieved by making
the transitional space 20 metres in length, gently ramping
towards the reception which was new architecture to
the rear of the landmark building. Moss green and cream
mosaic pattern continuing in the tradition of Roman
floors take you into the heart of the hotel.

Four specifically commissioned porcelain statutes of muses glazed in gold are mounted on plinths against the polished plaster wall. Art is integrated into the property as the client has a private modern collection including Roy Lichtenstein, Allen Jones, Steve Kaufman and Picasso, and acquired the Museum Hundertwasser House to add to his portfolio.

Central to the project is the rotunda of the reception—here a subtle glimpse of the coffered ceiling of the gallery is visible. Meanwhile the floor dominates the room. Taking its influences from beautifully patterned floors of the Pantheon in Rome and the Neues Museum in Berlin the colours are very rich: red and green marbles create a swirling teardrop and figure of eight pattern, muted by a French limestone is known as a "Klimt floor".

(overleaf) An S-shaped cabinet forms the
reception desk, filled with white bisque
by Nymphenburg, which snakes into the
reception room, where it is surrounded
by walls lined in soft, buttoned, luxurious
cream leather.

Harking back to the decadence to be found in the Austrian-Hungarian Summer and Winter palaces, flashes of brass-framed glass partitions and brass table pedestals imbue a grandeur found in nineteenth-century Viennese coffee houses, arranged to impress in a thoroughly modern La Véranda restaurant.

Glass mixed into polished plaster adds reflection where a crystal cut glass pendant makes a ghostly contour in the restrooms, creating soft light to illuminate the face.

For flamboyance, a brass swan neck is the faucet situated above a small brass bowl with a vanity unit made from Italian Portoro Oro marble from La Spezia. The plasticity of what is in effect secondary accommodation is continued by the carved gilded frames surrounding the mirrors.

A Roy Lichtenstein Pop art work hangs above the conference boardroom table and is reflected in the mirror on the facing wall. The room has a dedicated street entrance carefully planned to provide access to non-residents when a function is taking place.

Selecting pendants by Koloman Moser from 1904, handcrafted in Vienna, was an unusual departure for the architects who usually design all the furniture in their projects. Their inclusion reinforces the idea of the hotel being a place to admire art, Moser himself being an influential artist of the Vienna Secession Movement, whose first president was Gustav Klimt.

St Stephen's Cathedral's zig-zag
tiled roof is visible in the skyline
from the hotel.

In the public rooms, principal doors
with smiling soleil are panelled within
door leafs in gold lacquer, becoming
the graphic emblem of the hotel.

Looking from the rooftop of Sans Souci Hotel over the museum quarter, the November sun lights the silhouette of St Stephen's Cathedral spire and casts shadows upon the imposing domes of the Natural History and Art History buildings, which are symmetrically arranged around the Burrgarten. These museums were created to house the imperial collections and were part of the Hofburg Palace complex at the centre of Vienna.

Marquetry pale oak with sycamore flower inlay is the finish to the floor in this elaborate bar. A gilded chandelier is reflected in the mirror table tops.

Carlo Mollino 1950s chairs collide with antiques found by the architects, and Fratelli Boffi's domed hooded porter chairs, to create a filmic scene in this city with its wealth of culture. With a resemblance to state palace interiors, sensual velvets and mirror walls complete the *Galerie des Glaces*.

An amusing antique rocking chair
with cherubs carved into the arms
is poised in the centre of the room.

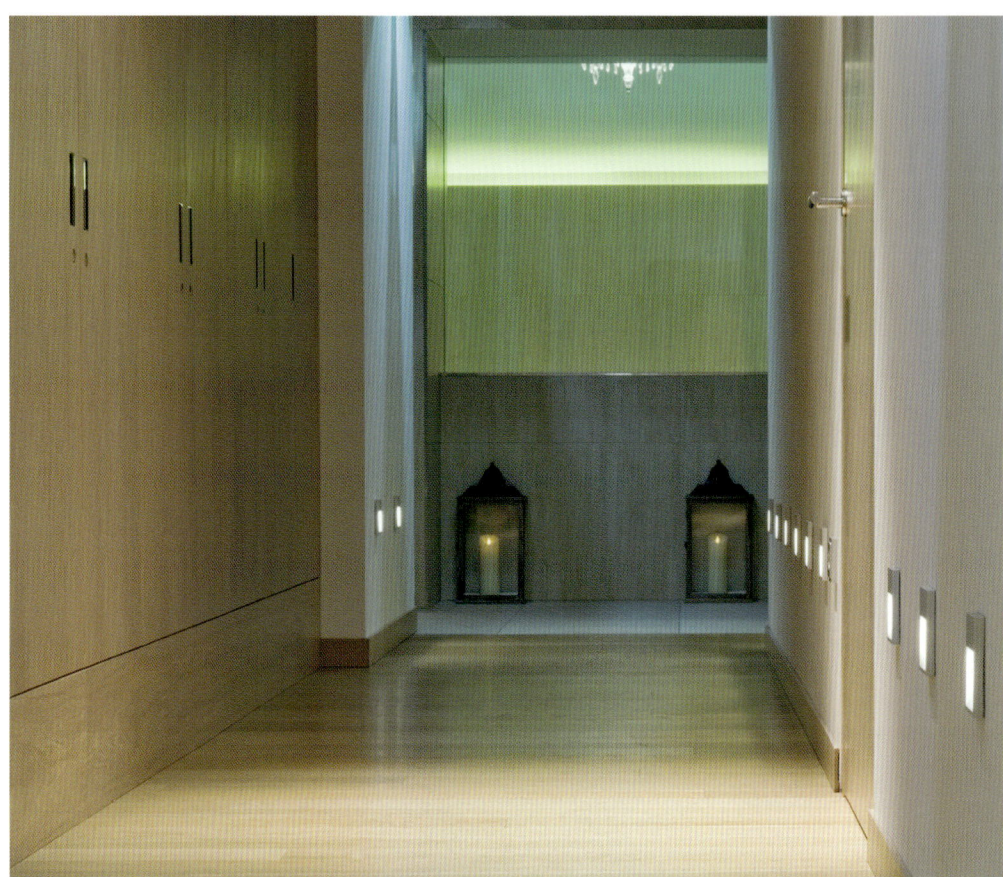

In the spa, cool air and contrasting light greets guests descending directly from the reception rotunda. Curved sycamore walls are well conceived to optimise space for the treatment rooms and relaxation suites.

Plunging into the lap pool that sits beneath original vaults, initially used as a cellar for the Hotel Høller, the waters are bright aqua. Stainless steel in a satin smooth resilient finish was chosen as a modern material for the pool, which contrasts with the ethereal qualities of the ancient travertine stone in the room.

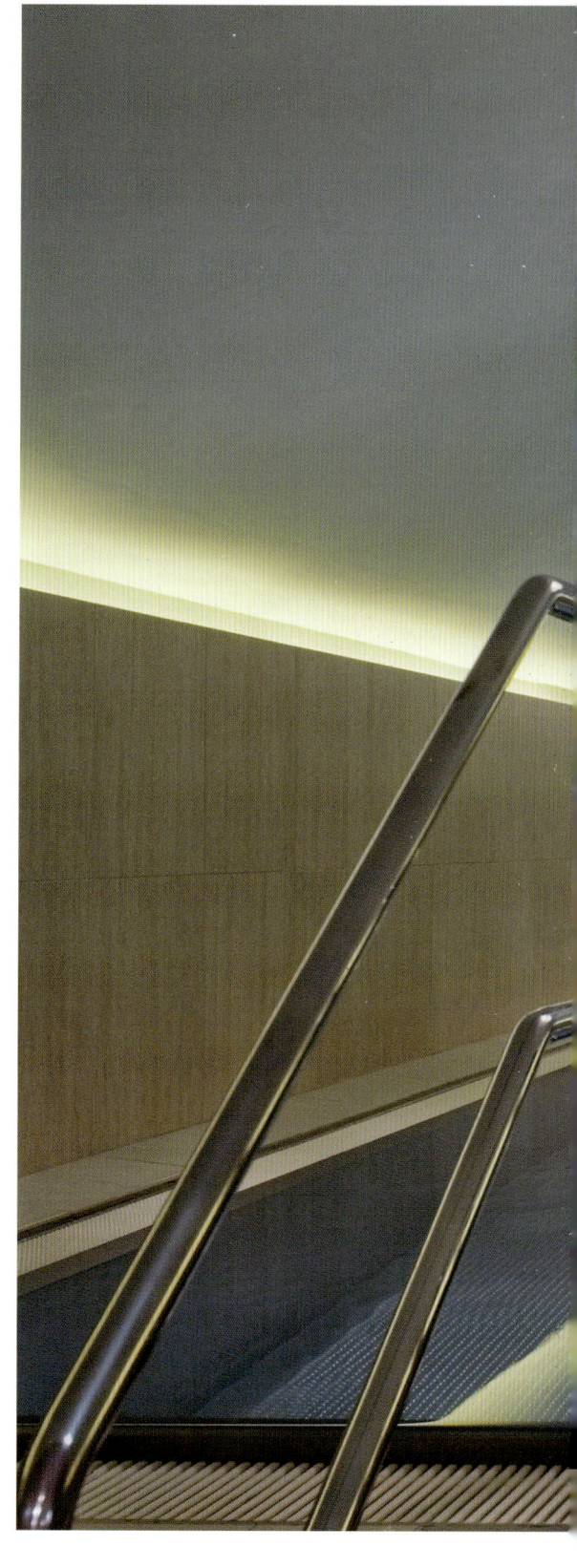

Here in the treatment rooms, decoration to the room is simple—sheer curtains and sycamore panelling to dado level, interrupted by the door height. Rooms are devoid of focal lights for peacefulness, with a lilac chaise upholstered for indulgence.

Clinical surfaces of acid-etched mirrored glass and polished stainless steel from a neutral background for the hues of the liquid spa products.

Washbasins are made from flamed stippled granite from Canada, and overlook a contemplation room, circular in plan, with an expansive curved cream leather banquette.

In the women's spa lounge low-level lighting glows, deep blue piping provides definition to the white waxed cotton cushions with primitive timber stools from Bali adding warmth to the minimal space.

Conventional Swedish
'his' and 'her' saunas are
a mirror image in plan.

To create the bedrooms, the architects drew on their love of marquetry, joinery and antiques in combination with their love of mid-century modern European furniture.

Entering the bathroom through
decorative doors, the room is
symmetrical with the tub being
in the centre of the door axis.

A simple occasional table is designed by the architects to complement the Gilda armchair manufactured in 1954, where a woollen fabric woven in Scotland on the Isle of Bute was chosen for the suite.

Room 123 is resplendently lit with a hand-blown lantern from England splitting the light into beams on the wall.

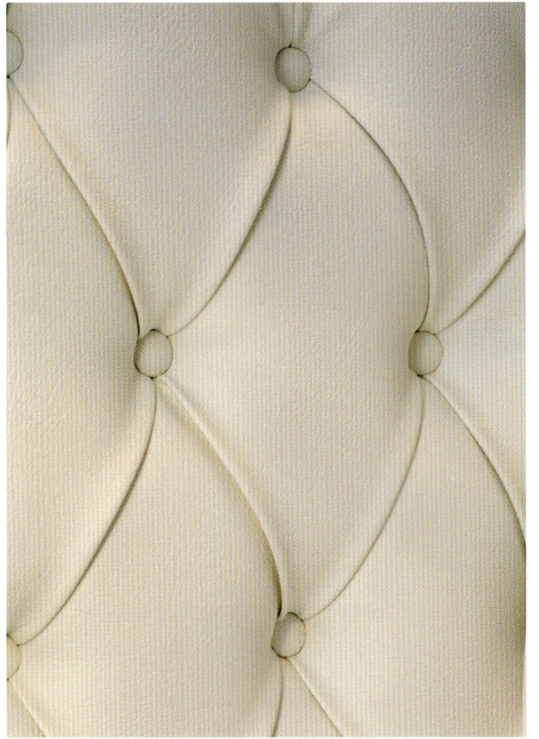

Beds are beautifully designed by the architects to be sumptuous; some have four posters for romance; others have wingbacks for a decadent stay. Each suite differs, which allows antiques and the owner's art collection to be dispersed across the hotel.

A silver 'signal' lamp collides in aesthetic
with the console; a handmade wall
mural is a modern take in the bedroom
design, an eighteenth-century Chinoiserie
embellishing the decoration.

In the dual aspect presidential suite, the bathroom is breathtaking. Art Deco in derivation, the circular room with a domed ceiling is lined in fluted glass rods, with vanities in polished Nero Marquina marble with chrome edges, small items in lapis blue marble for definition and completed with a decorative white pendant suspended above the bath.

(overleaf) A simple monastic spout is positioned on a chequerboard Carrera marble floor with a round bath the centrepiece of the room.

ADAM HOTEL CROATIA

Situated within the nineteenth-century garden quarter planned with a tree-lined avenue leading to Bacivice Beach, the site sits in close proximity to the Palace of Diocletian. The Adam Hotel faces the Adriatic coastline where the aromatic scent of cypress is always abundant. Entering an international architectural competition to create a new hotel, Archer Humphryes' entry was selected because it responded with an innovative urban resort. Formulating an approach to an untouched site is a complex task. Counter-intuitively, the client was seeking an exhibitionist solution to the brief; the architects resisted and began their own investigations to create a proposal derived from the cultural background of the site.

On the first trip to the city, visiting the Palace of Diocletian was a logical starting point. The way in which this city palace remains an inhabited palimpsest—core to the fabric of contemporary society, as well as being a living testament to Roman civilisation from almost two thousand years ago—completely entranced the architects. Since Emperor Diocletian's retirement to Split in 305 AD the Imperial 'castrum' and residence has been occupied continuously: from Byzantium rule to the more recent Socialist Yugoslavia. Romanesque, Renaissance and Baroque monuments have been embedded into the architecture within this ancient setting with the palace's peristyle being a modern urban square where everyone congregates at sundown in the city's 'heart'.

What was intriguing was the famous Scotsman Robert Adam's visit to the site as part of his Grand Tour in the eighteenth century. Adam's rediscovery of the legacy of the Tetrarch's architecture had a huge impact on his career and inspired his famous houses. Adam published his monumental work, *The Ruins of Spalatro*, in 1764.[6] Depicted within this scholarly work are the Ancient Egyptian architectural details whose origins can be traced back to Syria that Adam reinterpreted in his own body of work.

Being an avid collector of Adam's drawings, the client shared the rare book, *The Ruins of Spalatro*, with the architects before starting the project and the architects consequently named the hotel The Adam.

Glistening white Salona stone was chosen to create a pure cubic orthogonal architectural volume for the exterior of the hotel building, the same limestone used by the Romans. The building's orientation in plan mirrors the mansions on the facing avenue. A 'villa' upon a podium, its centre is a five-storey atrium, influenced by Diocletian's open-air Rotunda built from Roman bricks. This vertical void orientates all the hotel rooms and creates a rarefied top-lit room, acting as an internal courtyard that organises the internal and architectural structure of the spaces.

Further capturing the essence of the beach location is the use of bleached limed oak whose tactile texture is best experienced barefoot straight from the sea, with glass storm lanterns shimmering with candlelight at dusk. All the senses are awakened in the interior with light reflected from Venetian mirror design, Empire purple velvets in the upholstery, diaphanous white silk sheers softly pulsing in the breeze filtering the sunshine at the doorways, Roman bricks to the walls, Croatian black and white marbled floors, carved Egyptian rams heads in furniture details and, in the atrium, timber screens which can be repositioned across the changing day.

Like a Roman Bath, the subterranean level houses the spa. Two pools and the spa have recreated the ritual of bathing, where the visitor progresses through spaces that become increasingly hotter, to the frigidarium with its tank of cold water, the tepidarium and, finally, the caldarium (hot room). The pool, sitting within the Roman brick cloisters, reflects the chandeliers in its depths. Perched on the edge of the The Adam absorbing the Adriatic Sea spray at the roof level is the infinity pool where, at sundown, the sarcophagus 'bar' provides a party scene.

Sleeping quarters with sea views are inner sanctums of intimacy and peace within the project. They were conceived with bathing and sleeping being a principal activity in these rooms which have been organised with sliding pivot reeded glass doors to be pulled back to open up the bathroom and bedroom, breeze and sunlight being pulled into the room. Rooms are accessed from the atrium void, orienting the visitor to the centre of the complex, allowing an almost ceremonial procession outwards from the heart of the building.

Diocletian and Robert Adam have exerted considerable influence upon the city's history, home to the only Romanesque Imperial palace and sea fortress to be continuously occupied. The Adam Hotel has embraced the power of the urban morphology and this became a crucial part of the genesis of the design. What has been achieved with the project is a modern architecture that responds to the traditions and metropolitan organisation that has shaped this ancient city. The result is a geometric, iconic object, an orchestrated sequence of spaces that control the light to layer it through to the interior structure. The void at the heart of the project gives equal importance to the interior and exterior space, following the simplicity of form found in the Roman Rotunda in Diocletian's retirement residence.

Winning an international architecture
competition, the architects created a pristine
white Salona stone cubic building with a
top-lit central chamber in the UNESCO city
of Split, where strict urban masterplanning
criteria needed to be met.

Open air oculus in the dome of the rotunda of
Galerija in Diocletian's Palace. The architects stayed
next to the rotunda, at the Hotel Vestibul which is set
against the original Roman walls. This open room
influenced them to create a top-lit atrium to the
hotel and to use Roman bricks in the public areas as a
contemporary application of a historical material.

Lofty suites are designed with lime-washed oak wall panelling and herringbone parquet floors in this seaside environment. Ample bathing spaces, which are essential next to the Adriatic, imbue a relaxed seclusion in the depths of the bedrooms.

Descending into the pool, a spectacular cloistered room is suggestive of a Roman bath with a modern twist, using a large-scale Murano mirror centred in the perspective to reflect the vista, with stately chandeliers rippling against the water's surface and Roman bricks.

AFTER ADAM

While designing the furniture for the restaurant Plum & Spilt Milk at the Great Northern Hotel in London, Archer Humphryes Architects forged a fruitful partnership with Carlo Boffi, the grandson of the master *ébéniste* (cabinet maker) who founded the Fratelli Boffi furniture company in Italy. It was a natural progression to create a furniture collection together and the result was After Adam which, as the name suggests, pays homage to the great eighteenth-century Scottish architect Robert Adam.

Archer Humphryes has frequently developed products and furniture for the spaces it designs. Working with Italian furniture nobility Fratelli Boffi—which has an enviable reputation for artisanal skills, detailing and finishes—was a real treat. After Adam was an opportunity to combine the best of traditional craftsmanship with the practice's twenty-first-century zeal for modern furniture design, creating pieces that work equally well as ensembles or standalone pieces.

For the After Adam collection, the architects drew particular inspiration from two Adams-related field trips undertaken before they commenced the Great Northern Hotel project. The first was to Diocletian's Palace at Split in Croatia, a fourth century complex that formed part of Adam's Grand Tour in 1780. The second was to Kedleston Hall in Derbyshire, a Neo-Classical mansion designed by Adam in the 1760s for the Curzon family. Initially it was the curved wings, geometry and sculptural motifs that dazzled the architects' imaginations. Then at closer inspection, details from the Roman Emperor's palace at Split could be seen superimposed upon the architecture and laced through into the interiors onto exquisite furniture, produced by Chippendale and others, in what was then a modern Georgian style.

The Adam style, and the Georgian architecture that flowed from the Adam brothers was one of the first style movements that advocated the unity between architecture and interiors to create a singular approach, presenting spaces as homogenous. This approach to the seamless flow of internal and external spaces strikes a deep chord with Archer Humphryes and is an ongoing aspiration that flows between its projects.

On many of Archer Humphryes' early visits to the Boffi factory to develop After Adam, a loose quote from Mies van der Rohe was repeated to the architects: "A chair is a very difficult object. A skyscraper is almost easier. That is why Chippendale is famous."[7] Archer Humphryes rose to the challenge by responding enthusiastically to Boffi's expertise and passion for making. From the start of the collaboration, the conversations with the Boffi family focused on a tantalising array of forms and traditional techniques and how these could be applied in contemporary form to satisfy an audience interested in modern aesthetics.

As the prototypes took shape, everyone in the factory participated and passed comment on the refinement of the pieces, from the depth of the plump upholstery right down to the correct width of stitch for the fabric. The result is a collection of nearly 50 sculptural pieces with majestic forms in both scale and style accented with petite occasional tables and chairs with exquisite carving and inlay, which would not look out of place in any finely appointed room. From the silver inlay right down to the hand-embroidered leather upholstery by Roberta Boffi, the collection is characterised by Boffi's tremendous attention to detail and quality, and a shared desire to stay true to the spirit of the original design concept.

While steeped in heritage and proudly eccentric, After Adam nonetheless combines the rigorous geometric proportions of classically styled architecture with functionality and modern day comfort. Names of individual pieces such as Baron Tweedmouth, Countess of Home or Three Scotts Watch are intended to be an ironic touch, adding a hint of flamboyance and personality, as the narrative behind the individual pieces gradually reveal their stories, their inspiration and influences.

When it was launched at the Salone del Mobile in Milan in 2014, the opulent collection was presented against a dramatic, backlit backdrop of ebony boiserie panels, the exhibition also designed by Archer Humphryes. The Salone del Mobile publication at the fair launch described the entire effect as "luxury to simplicity" and the collection as "desire for distraction and uninhibited spatio-temporal incursions for a design that becomes a narrative".[8]

At the heart of the concept for After Adam is the desire to expand the repertoire of a modern collection by drawing on rare, traditional skills at a time when specialist trades are fast diminishing within the furniture industry as a whole. Plans are already afoot to add further pieces to the Fratelli Boffi collection, including a number of items using cane and weaving—another fading art form ripe for revitalisation for contemporary audiences.

Majestic candelabra in turned
natural oak are the sculptural
leitmotif of the collection.

Kimbolton Tall Boy in grey oak with flashes
of colour in the interior continues a heritage
of centuries of menusieurs whose expertise
and skill is slowly being eroded by mass
production as fewer and fewer craftsmen
enter apprenticeships to learn artisan trades
passed down through generations.

'Formidable Beast' armchair, in 'straw' coloured leather and lacquered oak with exquisite details in the rosette and beading, comes from a long lineage of Milanese manufacturers, which the architects were able to employ in each piece of the collection.

A solid leg post in grey oak contrasts with the delicate diagonal grain in four quadrants on the table top. The piece is called Four Tetrarchs, emulating the four co-emperors of the Roman Empire holding up Diocletian's authority, which interested the architects when they were given a tour by the state's archaeologist in Croatia to study the Roman palace.

Marquetry abstract flower motif set in
bronze is inlaid; a border with a rosette
paterae completes the credenza. A black and
white striped border has been compared to
Ettore Sottsass' Memphis group movement,
which has its origins in Milan.

Boiserie panelling with backlit laser cut pattern reflects dramatically against the ebony tall boys sides, where the chequer detail similar to the Kimbolton can be picked up in the foreground.

Three Scotts Watch benches in natural oak have individual carved roundels to the back with a traditional egg and dart border. This decoration is in stark contrast to the curved back on the reverse side which is smooth and minimal for comfort, adding a modern twist to the sculptural form.

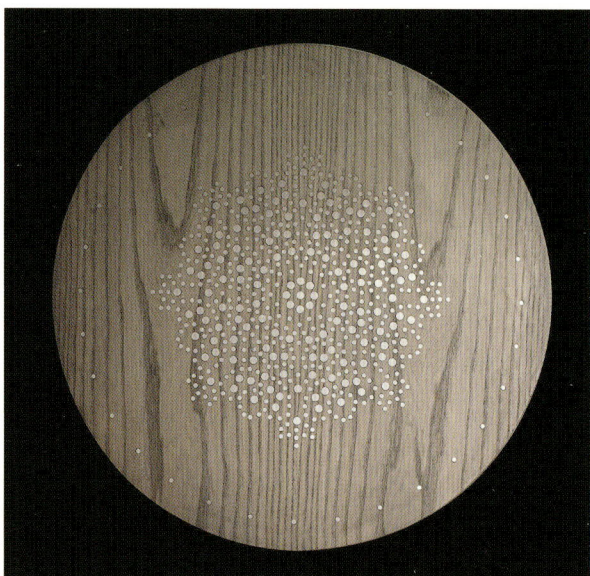

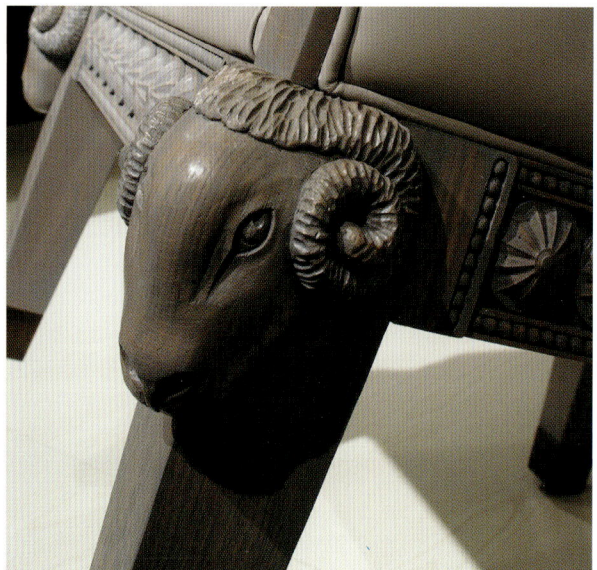

Here the architects combined stained black Beech timber edgings with English lime wash rubbed into the grain, providing texture to the ensemble of smooth Cordoba Black leather and nearly-black sheepskin to the upholstery of the theatrical Duchess of Home smoking chair. Its simple elegant lines mean that it would not look out of place against a rustic stone fireplace in a country home or in formal rooms in a contemporary town house.

Weathered grey oak circular table top with the chrysanthemum abstracted pattern inlaid with brushed stainless steel, adding a fragility to an otherwise utilitarian solid everyday functional item.

A carved Ovis head is a classical motif on the armchair leg. Popular in the eighteenth century after the excavation of Pompeii, it was an ironic reference to the classical origins adopted by Robert Adam, in this otherwise modern chair.

AFTER ADAM

Rosewood marquetry scribed with Tulip, Sycamore and
Cherry was the showstopper at Saloni del Mobile Milano.
A scallop-shaped table has a scale to seat 16. Formed as a
petal shape with an elliptical 'Bow Bench' to match, the
architects also added carved Sun or Moon chairs in white
washed oak and gloss mahogany. This ensemble was the
triumph of the show, exhibiting the guarded privileges
and secret techniques of the *ébéniste* artisans.

AFTER ADAM

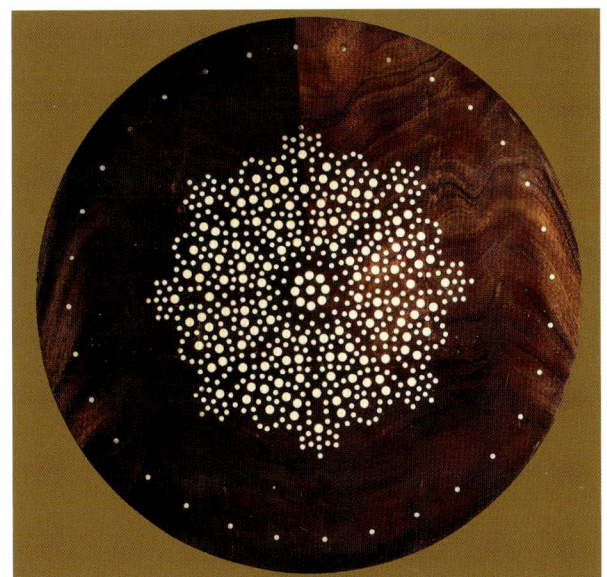

Golden Fleur, an occasional table with a pattern abstracted from a flower on a Kyoto kimono band, which the architects artistically reinterpreted into a graphic emblem—initially appearing in Aayas' pendants, then in The Beach in the Panton chairs' CNC cutting and now within the After Adam inlay ornamentation. This piece has a highly reflective luxurious surface with a sculptural pedestal turned from solid rosewood that complements many room compositions.

Reaffirming their collaboration with the Milanese company, Archer Humphryes once again design the stand and furniture for Salone del Mobile 2015. Entitled 'Four Quatrefoils' the ensemble includes high stools formed from blond limed oak and bleached cane with a decorative flower motif, and a table surface of quartz and inlaid bronze. Inspiration was found in the heavily decorated Gothic castles of Wales by William Burges, which the architects visited as field research for the public areas of St Pancras Renaissance Hotel for Harry Handelsman. A sharp contemporary twist is provided by the light flattened materials—where, traditionally, they would have been Jacobean oak with intricate edges. Dark timber forms the frame for circular mirrors on a black timber finished wall.

Juno and Jupiter floor lamps, rising to two
metres in height, are reminiscent of traditional
gas lanterns. Captured here are the reflections
that dance in the amber glass flask. Similar in
derivation to the incandescent delicate pendants
for the Plum & Spilt Milk restaurant in the Great
Northern Hotel, the scale is incongruent.

AAYA

Aaya was commissioned by the Yau family to be an authentic Japanese eatery; the result was described by Charles Campion of the *London Evening Standard Review* as: "Very polished indeed. The design makes you want to look through a Thesaurus for new words that say, 'lavish, posh and slick'. Upstairs there is a large cocktail bar with an array of glittering bottles and a dining room that looks good sized until you go downstairs and find one twice as big with what may be the swishiest sushi counter in London."⁹

Transforming what was an austere commercial space into a lush, sensuous, absorbing restaurant and bar seemed an impossible task, made more challenging by a remarkable client family that has defined Asian oriental eateries for decades following the creation of Wagamama and the Michelin star-awarded Hakkasan and Yauatcha. Above all else, the Yaus expected originality.

For answers, Archer Humphryes looked to the Far East—to Tokyo's Omotesando, shrines in Kyoto and, in particular, Nanzen Ji Zen Temple. An invitation at the beginning of the project to travel with the Yaus to explore regions of Japan was, for Archer Humphryes—who had some personal knowledge of Japanese culture having both been residents—an incredible, poignant start.

Influences as far-ranging as the sanctity of a Zen Buddhist Palace Temple, under a shower of cherry blossom, at the base of the Higashiyama Mountains—an enduring metaphor for the ephemeral nature of life—to the traditional performances of the Kabuki Theatre and the 'architectural showcase' streets of Omotesando on the way to the Meiji Shrine present an array of opposites. East and West, tradition and modernity, black and white were the components held in balance and harmony by the architects as the design was rigorously executed.

At the core of the design is the combination of these tantalising opposites. The staircase that connects the spaces is a starting point; a structural feat, it manipulates the vertical space through its diaphanous, diffused, lit structural glass wall and suspended stone treads, behaving like a lantern. Together the opposites represent a preciousness associated with exquisite jewellery and, at the same time, something rugged, constantly changing with the light. It evokes a Japanese aesthetic known as *Wabi-Sabi*, a concept of extreme refinement in which ideal beauty is generated by the collision of the imperfect or transient with an appreciation of the ingenuous integrity of natural objects and processes.

Taking its cue from nature, traditional Japanese patterns and materials are reinterpreted in a contemporary London dining experience suited to the febrile and composite nature of Soho. Diners' attentions are drawn to the bespoke embroidered lampshades displaying floral motifs drawn from the cummerbund of a Kimono found in Kyoto. The vibrant colours and the chrysanthemum pattern are imbued with symbolic meaning from as far back as the Edo period. Archer Humphryes transposed the traditional design, whose colours had a cosmological and a seasonal dimension. The lilac colour, which is the predominant colour for the embroidered lampshades suspended above the sushi bar, is associated with undying love, imagery derived from the fact that the murasaki plant used to create the dye has very long roots; the pink accents throughout the interior have a poetic reference connoting femininity, glamour, allure and, ultimately, cherry blossom: the beauty of living.

Carefully conceived to combine delicate surfaces, such as bronze screens with parchment set into them, contrasted with carved wood, utilising the chrysanthemum pattern monochromatically, scored within timber screens, linings and panels, a successful language for a meditative experience was created for the dining room. Warm expanses sensuously lit by fragile Japanese lanterns against the cold stone and solid white crystalline glass tables blur the boundaries between subtle contemporary lines and framed objects or materials passed down by generations.

A luminous horizontal space is defined by the ceiling, which has tatami matting suspended above the crystalline white stone floor, quintessentially Zen.

An expansive linear bar stretches along one length, defining the room. This monolith is reflected in the dramatic ribbed glass on the opposite wall, for visual perfection. The furniture, made by Cappellini in Italy, utilises the carefully created stripped bare palette of white, ebony and hot pink, to complete the room with absolute finesse.

A sumptuous blond wood room houses the enchanting sushi counter, an illuminated jewel at centre stage. The sushi masters themselves appear to have danced straight from the grandeur of a performance at the Kabuki Theatre. What has been achieved is a spectacle initiated by the Yaus' innovative desire to offer the ceremony of authentic eating in a divine dining room that is monastic in architectural order.

Over the length of the room, at the lower level, the architects introduced a crystalline white glass sushi counter as the main centrepiece to the blond panel enclosure. Silk pendants embroidered with golden and indigo flowers punctuate the monochromatic interior, their quatrefoil volume lined in pink adding a softness to this monastic restaurant. Pink repeats, and can be found on the leg struts of the benches and in the flesh of the sushi preparation where the chefs work.

Conceptually, the bronze, steel
and stone staircase was seen
as a lit lantern connecting the
floors of the restaurant.

Glass bronze screens with LED internal illumination form the palette for multiple grid matrix partitions, following the tradition of screen construction in Japanese houses or temples, which the architects visited in the shrines of Kyoto, particularly within the Sagano bamboo forest. Instead of paper in the sliding frames of the monuments, fluted glass adds translucency that radiates light into the depth of the restaurant in a contemporary reinterpretation.

A lantern manufactured from parchment paper and wire mesh is designed with orthogonal lines and a candlelit glow to emulate authentic Japanese building materials.

Tatami mats on the ceiling are an unexpected placement of the material. They add acoustic benefits in a grid arrangement between oak beams and conceal the ceiling's real use as a complex heating, cooling and accessible lighting arrangement. A combination of the rustic and engineering principles are Japanese themes of *Shibui*, where design is intended to be unobtrusive and subtle.

Through the bronze stair frame enclosure flashes of pink pervade. When combined with black and lilac—found on the dark leather of the refectory benches and the lilac of the damask silk embroidery—pink is meant to imbue seduction in Japanese culture.

186   AAYA

Chrysanthemums scored into oak add a decorative relief to panels and doors which otherwise have no expressed detail in the joinery.

Tatami ceiling matt made from rice straw, plaster moulding for bronze entrance door knob in production, understated chiselled signage inscribed in Portland Stone, embroidery derived from the Kimono band, stitched by the Maharishi fashion brand in Hong Kong from exquisitely executed original art work from the architects.

Square Bronze pull plate with rebated
quatrefoil door handle mimics the plan of
the embroidered pendant drum and is the
only detail on the minimal door leaf.

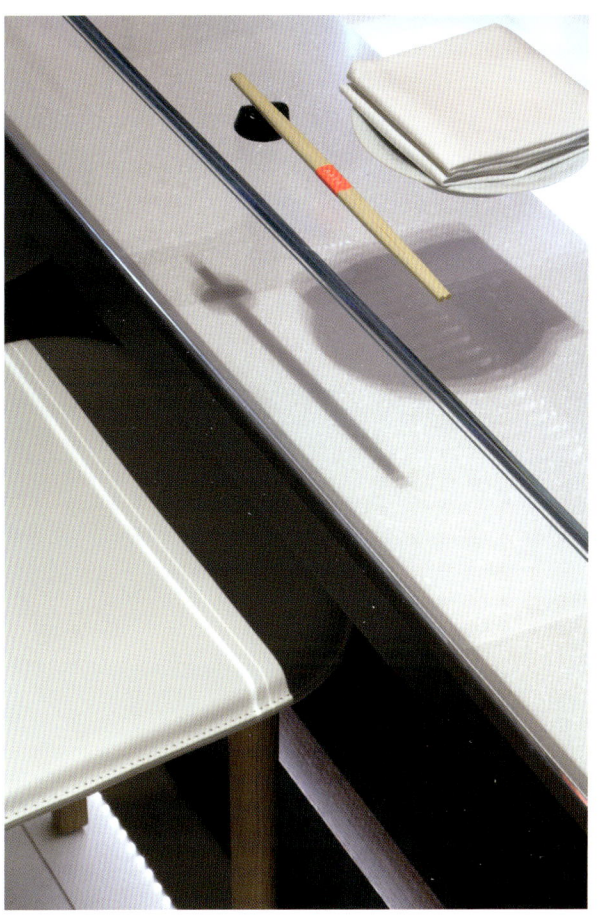

Ebony panelled walls are striking, adding drama to the
ground floor restaurant and bar. Here the relief of the
chrysanthemums is subtle against the sharp contrast of
the opaline white table tops, which stand out against the
walls. Table settings add a further layer to the design and
are predominantly white and austerely arranged, with
natural bamboo chopsticks and 'hot pink' wrapping.

Washing areas take their language from traditional Japanese Onsens. A simple spout made from bronze takes its proportion from bamboo. A black slate backsplash completes the scene indicative of exterior hot spring baths. Signage to the restrooms continues the simple graphics using the material palette of the interior.

NATIONAL CAFE TERRACE

Trafalgar Square—one of the world's most famous urban squares and a focal point for numerous events in history—is home to the National Cafe Terrace. The illustrious impression of *The Battle of Trafalgar* by JMW Turner, 'the painter of light', was considered controversial upon its completion. Its symbolical narrative denied a sequential reading of the events that took place, instead fusing them into a singular allusive image. After victory in the 1805 Napoleonic wars, the Royal Navy wanted to be glorified and, in the opinion of the presiding government, Turner's painting was an embarrassment to 'the Establishment'. For Nelson, "who exercised and demanded patriotic duty and valued its rewards", his own death in the battle constituted the ultimate act.[10] Turner's painting was seen to undermine this by not honouring the palm of victory belonging to those whose "sense of duty and commitment is greatest".[11]

The National Cafe Terrace, developed for Peyton and Byrne by Archer Humphryes with the Gallery trustees, has a triumphant position, symmetrically placed either side of the National Gallery on the northern side of Trafalgar Square. The City of Westminster granted permission to the practice's proposal in 2010 after a careful evaluation of English Heritage's protection of the Gallery and the need for commerce by the clients. Arguably central London's pre-eminent gathering place, the square sees millions of visitors annually mingling between the two majestic fountains. As well as the iconic Nelson's Column—a monument that was chosen by competition, selected by the Duke of Wellington—four plinths dominate the square. Three support statues, while the fourth famously remains 'empty' to a permanent piece. Currently, artworks appear on the plinth on a rotating basis, drawn from competitions and the will of the serving public authority. The fourth plinth sits immediately adjacent to the National Cafe Terrace. The positions of all the monuments around the square had to be respected, with the architects taking a sensitive view as to the insertion of the cafe into this public realm, to maintain key sightlines, newly achieved pedestrian activities and ultimately the visual prominence and ascendance of Wilkins' purpose-built gallery.

Trafalgar Square's current iteration was devised by a team led by Foster + Partners in "World Squares for All", when the north side of

the square was closed to traffic, providing a ceremonial frontage to the gallery. This return to civic space provided the opportunity for the architects to generate a new position for the Cafe Terrace, linked to the main square via Foster+Partners' enlargement of the public space.

Initially operating in the summer months through 2011 and 2012, the cafe seated 96 diners. Proportion and scale were incredibly important in the derivation of the design, not to be visible against the box planting raised area or conceal the windows and columns of the gallery: it should appear almost invisible against the backdrop of the prominent architecture and openness of the square. Detailed thought was given to the furniture and carefully designed canopies, which had to satisfy the concerns of English Heritage and the trustees. The vast retractable canopies do not interrupt the facade of Wilkins' masterpiece, or occlude the view of Nelson's Column, despite providing important respite from the sun in the summer months. A unique experience that has never before existed in the square's history, the architect's design is divided between two pavilions, which sit comfortably either side of the Grade I listed gallery entrance. Before final approvals, the design had to take into account the listed statue of George Washington, by not obscuring it through the architectural additions, thus letting it remain in full view against its existing backdrop of the National Gallery's south pavilion.

Overall, the radical reworking of the public realm at Trafalgar Square has been a success story for the arts. The public world stage has returned to the heart of the city and Archer Humphryes has provided a civic cafe from which to witness the vivacity of the *teatro mundi* where strangers mix in the disorder. "Society is a theatre. All men are actors", wrote Richard Sennett in his 1974 *The Fall of Public Man* which atomised the self-absorption of the inwardly 'me generation', taking life away from our urban existence as more and more public space became populated by bureaucracy, and privatised.[12] Even when Turner created his representation of Nelson's victory, spaces and images were being politicised, in their rendition of reality. The square, and the arts, are vital components of the city, even when the space becomes a political place infused with ideals and memories of the civic state.

William Wilkins principal facade from 1832–1838 remains relatively unchanged in symmetry since it was first built. The image shows the terrace of the National Cafe to the right of the portico, the only visible manifestation being the box hedging and canopies carefully concealed by the architects in order to secure the complicated consents for the adaptation to the landmark building, realising an external room for a 100 diners.

ISARN

French nineteenth-century explorer Auguste Pavie remarked of Isarn:

> Conquered and charmed, an impression remains with me: rafts crossing noisily over the Nam Khan's rapids into the Mekong; white and gold pagodas roofed with coloured varnished tiles; tall houses built in wood and huts constructed with palm leaves, their roofs covered with thin strips of bamboo; steeply rising banks between small gardens and providing an appropriate splash of colour.[13]

Isarn is located in the northeast of Thailand on the Khorat Plateau. The Khmer Empire once ruled this area, with Siam and Laos of French Indochina taking control at different points in history until the national government claimed it back in the mid-twentieth century. The name "Isarn" was derived from Isana, a manifestation of Shiva as deity of the northeast asserted during Thaification. She has "invisible power that governs the universe" with north and east representing water and air, respectively.[14] Whether this interpretation of the goddess is accepted, or not, the area's cuisine is distinct certainly from the central Thai palate, and the menu of the restaurant Isarn reflects this with offerings such as coconut sticky rice, green papaya salad and sumptuous desserts from the region. Such attention to detail in the food is to be expected; co-owner Tina Juengsoongneun is Alan Yau's sister.

Informed by designs that the architects had previously completed for the Yaus, Isarn began as a neighbourhood eatery, providing a welcome antidote to the exploding market of chain restaurants on Islington's popular Upper Street. The restaurant occupies a restricted linear site, which required ingenuity on the part of the architects to achieve a functional and inviting dining interior. Described by *Time Out* as possessing a "slinky, contemporary decor, with dark wood and oversized lampshades, which gives Isarn a polished, expensive image".[15]

By controlling the perspective, the architects made a virtue of the long narrow site (four metres wide by 23 metres long). Linking four areas—the street elevation, the bar, the conservatory and the courtyard—like a 'river' without interruptions or barriers, was the simple solution that provides an atmospheric and vivacious space, with a canopied roof giving a sense of heightened volume, despite its diminutive actual size.

Natural sailcloth for the canopy stretches overhead suspended in the 'air', imitating the traditional rafts with their makeshift masts crossing the Mekong through the depth of the restaurant. Contrasting with the ebony vertical planked timber walls—which resemble the boarding of traditional 'shop-houses' in the villages of the Khorat Plateau—the two opposites suspend the space between notions of the transient and permanent. As expressed by Baudelaire: "Modernity is the transient, the fleeting, the contingent; it is one half of art, the other being the eternal and the immovable."[16] Unified by the choice of a monochromatic palette of classic materials, the dichotomous relationship of the lightweight fabric that absorbs sound and the wrapped black timber textured envelope of the rooms' walls becomes alive with accents of precious decorative points of light, that equally represent the interplay of light and dark. The inspiration for the lighting design was the Candle Festival, which marks the start of Vassa in July in Ubon. Lighting designer Jonathan Cole made the pendant pieces for the architects. Having shared studio space with Archer Humphryes in the past, he was able to execute the designs in tandem with the evolution of the overall concept, which added dynamism to the lights—a prominent part of the scheme.

Pendants float apparently effortlessly in the space. Two pendant designs are predominant: one is small and focused in scale with patterns carefully cut into delicate folded black metal; the other is a frangible translucent parchment paper—a bright white Thai lantern. Both are adorned with a butterfly design that, within the metal pendant, creates a silhouette with beams of refracted light, spinning against the background walls. In contrast, the paper lanterns create an ambient stream of light, softly radiating. Butterflies often represent rebirth in artistic symbolism; the butterfly was the only ornamentation that Archer Humphryes introduced within the otherwise modern interior. Representing a fleeting moment, the butterflies and light are moments draped in the solidity of the architecture. Like the mystery of the Mekong Lights, which sparkle across the water in the darkness, the lanterns in the restaurant's long narrow space provide stark, dazzling brightness against the dark walls, suspended in space and time. The impression that is left is captured by Haruki Murakami (村上春樹): "Hundreds of butterflies flitted in and out of sight like short-lived punctuation marks in a stream of consciousness without beginning or end."[17]

Basket weave banquettes in a dark brown leather lattice against a sawn ebony vertical timber wall finish run the length of the this narrow eatery. It is imbued with the details found in vernacular buildings of fishing villages and floating vessels of the Tonle Sap Lake in Cambodia and Thailand, visited by the architects.

Butterflies laser-cut into bronze drums create patterns on the walls and tables— reminiscent of a carousel, the impermanence of the light flickers on the regular white square mosaic tiles.

Paper lanterns delicately adorned with butterflies are made to appear as a repeating shadow puppet. The wings are domestic in scale and have the appearance of being homemade.

CÂY TRE

Cây Tre Soho is the first French Vietnamese cafe to open in Soho. It is part of the Vietnamese Kitchen group, which has branches in Hoxton and Shoreditch. It is just what you might imagine a Vietnamese restaurant in Soho to be like: "chic, minimal decor, impeccably smart and efficient black-clad staff, beautifully serving food. Customers are very mixed—tourists, Chinatown youngsters looking for something fresh, and a smattering of techies and media types".[18] Kêu! Banh Mi Deli was the first project Archer Humphryes completed for the client, beginning the material palette and identity that flows through all the subsequent commissions.

With each new project Archer Humphryes takes note of every aspect of the project: location, scale, client, identity. This project was no exception. From directing the graphics, to signage, to the uniforms and the 'objets trouvés' in the interiors, a seamless proposition was given to the client that extends beyond the architectural and interior design, becoming entrenched in the genesis of the entire experience of the restaurant, appealing to the audience of diners. Simply described, the brief was to create an interior in which this popular cuisine could be enjoyed easily throughout the day and evening. Anything made for the projects is an expression of the client's intentions through the eyes of the architects, even when that is unknown at commencement. All restaurants or hotels are similar in their basic form; they are shaped to realistically reflect the facts of the cultural authenticity of the brief even where fantasy is engaged. In a neighbourhood like Soho where eating is commodified and there is a multitude of cuisines from every continent to choose from, it is a very difficult premise for architects to foster, impose and present possibilities. Archer Humphryes always endeavours to transcend the client's expectations in its capacity to imagine spaces, subverting the established prevalent cultural response. Cây Tre Soho prides itself on using fresh, local ingredients with impeccable provenance—witness the delectable Devon crab wrap with crisp lettuce and perilla leaves or grilled Cornish scallops in spring onion oil on the menu. This, combined with the architects' ability to practically fulfil the ambitions for the project, is what distinguishes it from any other scenario in the neighbourhood.

A recent trip to Tonlé Sap, the largest freshwater lake in South East Asia, was a good departure point for thinking about the opportunities for the project. Unusually it is a river that reverses its flow from the Himalayas to the Mekong, marked by the Water and Moon Festival during the open fishing season. Vietnamese live within floating villages. From pagodas on the banks, with Cambodians, together they carve sacred canoes from singular 'coki', trees during the festival that are then painted colourfully.

The walls of Cây Tre are lined in sand-blasted Douglas Fir timber boards and the floors' patterned mosaics incorporate crushed white marble tiles: a deliberately simple aesthetic, which followed the vernacular timber floating homes set against the stillness of the lake that Archer Humphryes had recently visited in Cambodia.

A long solid block, the bar is formed in black cracked glazed volcanic stone and sits in the cafe entrance. The bar contrasts with the overwhelming black and white geometric graphic pattern of the door. Black stained English oak and soft black leather furniture sit in silhouette against the cool finishes and careful atmospheric lighting. Reflecting off the floor, the back bar and the numerous glass surfaces, the light resonates in the space.

Seating almost 100, the restaurant is set out with high tables arranged opposite the bar, with cafe seating organised along the length of the restaurant; more formal seating is set out in the dining room at the rear of the space. Everything is conceived and designed by the architects.

Intense saturated colour is found in the staircases and bathrooms. Vivid, luminous, coloured pattern is applied to the menus and uniforms providing an explosive blast against the monochromatic geometric architectural aesthetic. Striking colours are reminiscent of the floating villages reflected in Tonlé Sap.

The architects' role is not to be an elitist in mass culture but to be humble. In this instance, in a place like Soho where everything competes and jostles for recognition, Archer Humphryes has imposed its own possibilities for the project, reached by reacting against a culture today which has a tendency to be infected with sameness. As Friedrich Nietzsche said, "In constructing concepts, we overlook that no two things are the same. There is no such thing as the concept of the leaf, only billions and billions of leaves."[19]

Cement graphic tiles form a runway from the exterior
street into the interior of the restaurant in the heart
of Soho. Monochromatic black and white marquetry
marks the entrance door, with the same pattern
repeated on the floor tiles at a smaller scale creating
a striking street frontage with minimal signage.

Douglas Fir treated with lime-washed oil from Scandinavia forms an enclosure to the room that is both aromatic and absorbs sound. Lining restaurants in timber is a recurring *au courant* for the architects.

Glazed volvic lava stone from Mount Etna is used to create a monolithic bar and high table top which is lustrous when polished and sealed.

Golden bell pendant lamps designed for the
famous Savoy restaurant in Helsinki add
shimmer to the black and white interior,
and follow the rhythm of the table places.

NAAMYAA

In Bangkok, the 'oriental city', and home to conspicuous consumption "not much between despair and ecstasy", street cafes and illicit vendors are the residents' mainstay.[20] In his quest for authenticity, Alan Yau's brief was to recreate the vivid street life of an Eastern eatery in a Western cityscape, as a surreal dreamscape. A personal friend of Archer Humphryes for two decades, having first met at the Felix bar in Hong Kong, then faithfully working together on the Hakkasan and Busaba Eathai concepts, it seemed a logical step for Alan Yau to appoint the architects to create this idea; suspended between vivid opposites of chaos and order, it was to be a challenging test for the practice.

Along with an eclectic collision of East and West in the dining experience, the architects had strict constraints that Yau expected from the design concept. Having been ordained as Buddhist Monk at Wat Dhammakaya before starting Naamyaa, it was no small pressure for the architects to come up with a quite different but equally memorable design for Yau for this Thai all-day cafe.

Wisely, they did not overplay the Siam influence, opting instead to create a cultural identity for the restaurant in its London location: something that they have been very agile at doing successfully for projects across the globe. The result at Naamyaa is a 'Pagan Temple' that has been described as exotic and inscrutable. As in Somerset Maugham's vivid journey from the mountains to Bangkok described in *The Gentleman in the Parlour*, it brings a lost world to life, as the architects' concept brings to life an evocative pipe dream of the East, without the illicit reality.[21]

Central to the concept is the kitchen which, with the bar, is the heart of the project. Dominating the room, the experience is reminiscent of the Thai street theatre that captivates its paying public. Oblique views are directed through the 'neon' glow of the glass kitchen cube, while highly textural screens across the cafe create simultaneously the illusion of openness and isolation for the voyeuristic diner.

These filmic views start from the exterior streetscape of the cafe where creating an arresting frontage with the facade of full-height, reflective black glass within a commercial building was a technical challenge for the architects. They succeeded, placing a light metal lattice screen behind the glass facade and dramatic illumination that one might not find out of

place in a Bangkok backstreet. Either side of the illuminated screens and the glass, people are the shadow theatre, providing a continual play of undulating movement against a *moiré* pattern.

This movement and activity is amplified intensely by the use of vertical columns of perpetual LED displays, which create a fractal pattern of Thai ornamentation, along with carefully controlled high-tech rotating fans. A visual spectacle is achieved, which provides the surrealism demanded by the brief.

Back in the interior the flanking walls are decorated in Thai materials and patterns that create an exploded rhythm. Along the back wall—or 'proscenium'—a three-dimensional topography is formed by using stacks of distinctive highly textural Thai bricks crowned with Golden Buddhas. Rich in materials, the golden deities create a 'casual religious' experience with dining which parallels closely Thai culture where the everyday relationship between life and Buddha is visually understood.

Archer Humphryes Architects—as always—were closely involved in the graphic content of the design which, in this concept, has been unusually expressed within a *toile de jouy* idea printed onto glazed ceramic tiles. A scene depicts a traditional activity taken from Thai narrative paintings, executed monochromatically in red and white— the colour red, when combined with white, symbolising joy in Thai culture. Abstracting this pattern into a continuous and disorientating graphic was a deliberate choice by the architects in order to create a shock within the diminutive space.

The success of the project is in its mystery of indecipherability, the starting point being a suspension between chaos and order, concentrating the mind on the present moment, arrested in time, as if on a journey through the night scene in an Oriental city.

As Somerset Maugham wrote upon arriving in Bangkok: "If you are interested in human nature, it is one of the greatest pleasures of travel."[22] Alan Yau's critical command as a restaurateur *par excellence* sees him constantly 'trawling the globe' in search of creative inspiration and authenticity to bring to his dining experiences; Naamyaa is no exception. The architects share Yau's passion for encountering and imagining the unknown, both in their friendship and the work they do together.

Central to the room is the kitchen in the open-plan restaurant. Furniture is made in complementary colours of red and sage, with cane running through the interior in this all-day dining experience. Strip baton lights invisibly suspended from the lofty ceilings along the facade characterise a Thai cafe's informality and equally allow strong visibility of the interior from the outside.

Terrazzo is used for the bar construction
and the floor finishes, in a neutral tone.
Eating takes place directly at the counter
where bright red high stools are set out.

Traditional Thai bricks imported from Ayutthaya form the defining wall in the interior, running the breadth of the restaurant, encapsulating an earthy element in the irregular relief like an old city wall. Hundreds of Thai golden deities from a temple in Thailand crown the wall.

Red neon LED signage is striking
against the Angel building's
dark glass and cladding, recently
Stirling prize-nominated.

A tiled Thai *toile* depicting scenes from art imagery found in classical Thai temples; an angel, forests and animals are graphically printed onto a Johnston white ceramic and greet guests when they enter.

In the restrooms the architects chose a repeat primitive pattern of bright blue and white, custom printed onto the tiles, generating a graphic quality to the functional facilities.

Glowing outwards, the glass facade frontage offers no concealment of the vibrant food spot where David Thompson, the chef who was awarded the first Michelin star in Europe for a Thai restaurant, lent his experience of Bangkok street stall culture to the menu.

BUSABA EATHAI GROUP

A name derived from Thai flora, Busaba Eathai has become an institution wherever it is set, with a tribal following of 'locals', some of whom choose to sit at the window seats, where they can watch the hustle of the surroundings with an al fresco feeling.

In recent Restaurant and Bar Awards, Archer Humphryes won top prize for the Bicester Village location. It was a brave decision to place the highly individual restaurant, described as being "like a cross between Far Eastern wooded simplicity and the upturned hull of a vast Viking warship" into a dense retail environment outside London.[23] Busaba says, "Design is a catalyst for a good atmosphere. A restaurant's primary business is with the food."[24] For the architects, resolution of the architectural interior is achieved when the content is fully rationalised in order for the spatial hierarchy to be interpreted successfully. Once this is attained it then forms the foundation for an energetic environment that can be conjured through the materiality of the place.

Archer Humphryes was involved in the early architectural concept for the first Busaba in London's Wardour Street, where the feted French designer Christian Liagre set out to take Thai food in a stylish setting to the masses, with the furniture design he created for the architectural concept. "Shared seating around square wooden tables met with an affordable menu of updated takes on classic Thai flavours in a setting that managed to capture the spirit of old Siam, whilst remaining unmistakably modern", describes the early version of the multiple restaurant.[25] Having completed over ten Busaba Eathai for the Yau family, the practice aims for each iteration to be individual, based upon the specifics of its location, yet at the same time embryonic of the first Wardour Street site. The architects' pragmatic and ordered response to rethinking the core concepts on every occasion maintains the restaurant's origins, not as a clone or a carbon copy, but as a member with its own 'following' and its own virtues that make it truly individual in the group. The latest addition by Archer Humphryes to the group will be in Dubai.

Employing the services of Australian chef David Thompson, a leading authority on Thai cookery, combines the Yaus' passion for authenticity with a twist from the Sydney chef from a Western perspective:

Thai food isn't about simplicity. It's about the juggling of disparate elements to create a harmonious finish. Like a complex musical chord, it's got to have a smooth surface but it doesn't matter what's happening underneath. Simplicity isn't the dictum here, at all. Some Westerners think it's a jumble of flavours, but to a Thai that's important, it's the complexity they delight in.[26]

The architectural interior mirrors this notion: spaces that connect everything into a 'simple' refectory mood, with rich materials that have, collectively, a combined refinement. Close up, a defining aspect of the design is the intricate detailing that is precisely constructed. Walls are lined in stained rattan, beams with hard wood purlins, boarding, bronze panels at low level, bars and pantries are detailed in black slates, dark colours are retained creating a glowing ambience. Continuing the radiance are the paper lampshades, providing scale and flattering light above the teak tables that are pegged together like 'Viking' vessels each able to seat ten strangers together. All materials collide to bring the tradition of Thai design that Archer Humphryes has reinvented into a Western modern affair.

The approach to each site looks at volume, entrances, balconies and dramatic staircases to generate a central energy to the design. Some of the locations have terraces and dining areas, whilst others have pools containing lilies and are planted with Frangipani trees. All venerate the Golden Buddha, which is given a symbolic prominent position upon arriving, an implicit part of Thai ceremony.

The Independent newspaper asked: "So where do you stand? Is restaurant design another part of the entertainment or do you want to be able to concentrate on what's on your plate and your companions?"[27] For the architects, a restaurant may be an opportunity for innovative experimentation that manifests itself as a statement space with the introduction of theatrical flourishes. In approaching restaurant design, Archer Humphryes has developed many different eating experiences. Having a nihilistic aversion to the 'vagaries of fashion', the practice aims to embody a motive in each architectural design that reaches beyond the superficial. As each new entrepreneur enlists film directors or fashion designers to create the latest sensation, it is sometimes more enjoyable to have a secular experience through which it is possible to concentrate upon the basic human needs of socialising and eating without interference from overpowering design. As it is a primeval urge to eat, it is decadence that explains the explosion of eating out in 'extreme interiors', with many people never learning to cook. One constant remains: all over the world we join one another to eat together in a place.

Modelled on a Thai longhouse, the architecture is made from *iroko* timber and is cleverly contained within the banal steel barn structures of Bicester Village. Incredulously the architects have taken the unimaginative site and transformed the nine-metre double-height volume into a multiple award-winning design and destination.

Working for ten years on the canteen style inspired concept restaurant, each site has its own vocabulary. At Panton Street, next to Leicester Square, a traditional teak lattice is placed at the entrance foyer where a Buddha is displayed and greets the visitor. Buddha's placement is a commonality across projects.

Square geometric tables made of teak set out on polished concrete are the mainstay of the convivial communal eating. They accentuate the smooth *iroko* panelling, partitions and balustrades.

Buddha is at eye level opposite the visitor on arrival in an auspicious position of the 'major chi entrance', an enshrinement that releases negative energy and brings positive forces into the establishment. Monks bless the space before trading.

Intricate details of candle flasks, graphic humour in restroom signage, and a Gio Ponti inspired coat hook.

Sir Albert Richardson is revered for his synthesis of traditional and modern approaches as a post-war traditionalist; one of his now listed buildings from the 1950s is the site of Busaba Panton Street. Requiring retention of timber sashes and venetian windows the facade was beautifully updated and remodelled by the architects.

The bronze trays with floating hot pink and white Gerberas have their origins in the Thai festival of Loi Krathong, where floating baskets are placed in the river when there is a full moon in the twelfth month of the Thai lunar calendar.

A solid carved timber stool is placed in
the window for individual dining, with
slate and teak lining to the walls.

The Busaba Eathai Bicester entrance has varnished rattan wall linings for texture. A sleek rendition of the Thai longhouse with a frameless glass door and bronze strap handle achieves a contemporary simplicity here, with Buddha looking on.

Infinite reflections in the mirror at the mezzanine level reveal the nine-metre gable roof structure lined in timber.

DUCK AND RICE

The pub is a quintessentially British expression of culture. This most venerated form of drinking establishment has its roots in the Copper Age of 3500–2300 BC and later in Roman civilization as a 'taberna' within an indoor market. Some began as coaching inns, others as alehouses selling beer as a necessary alternative to drinking contaminated water. Taverns however sold only wine and were fashionable places to meet. Architecturally lavish gin-shops began to appear in Regency England, the age of elegance and decadence. "These new products were employed to the full, creating a dazzling spectacle of light and reflection. They stood out in the dark streets like beacons. To the poor they were palaces— Gin Palaces."[28] All bars, pubs and restaurants have emerged from this balance of human necessity and exuberance in society. The gastropub is no exception. This developed in the early 1990s when food became a core experience of the pub as brewers sought to reinvigorate their flagging industry.

Archer Humphryes Architects has designed more than 40 restaurants but the most recent one, The Duck and Rice, is definitely their first Cantonese gastropub, combining British and Chinese themes of dining and drinking.

The Duck and Rice was created in the former Endurance Pub, a Berwick Street boozer in London's Soho. The fusion concept was conceived with restaurateur Alan Yau, a longstanding Archer Humphryes client since 1998, and marks Yau's first return to Chinese cooking in over a decade since the successes of Hakkasan and Yauatcha. A simple brief combining a traditional pub scene with craft beers and Chinese cuisine was the blueprint of the design and Archer Humphryes resultant reinvention creates a thoroughly modern venue out of this traditional hard-drinking den.

To do this, Archer Humphryes stripped the 1960s pub right back to its concrete frame, completely rebuilding the architecture with beautiful, black handmade brickwork, and putting in an extraordinary new window system—symmetrical and freestanding in expression with an abstract trapezoidal pattern created with random screens of transparent and milk glass set within a large bronze anodized frame. Curved and capable of sliding, these screens dominate the interior—bringing in brightness and exuding a light luminance onto the market streetscape. Like the gin palaces that preceded the modern bar, its feverish display is intended to entice people in for shelter.

Inside, a Western, occidental atmosphere emanates, with guests greeted by the sounds of drinking and conversation from the main pub bar, which occupies the ground floor. To achieve this ambience, Archer Humphryes placed the kitchens off-stage entirely, with dining for 70 located on the first floor, cantilevered over the front door.

The Duck and Rice has many of the hallmarks of a traditional tavern including dark oak finishes and doors that mimic the simplicity of Elizabethan joinery with the suggestion of heavy iron hinges from a local forge. To emphasise the craft beer element, smooth, reflective copper tanks containing unpasteurised beer with a shelf life of five days are made prominent at the entrance. These, along with traditional beer taps and pumps on the bar top, clearly orientate the customer on arrival.

An industrial iron circular staircase connects the two customer spaces, manufactured to the architects' specification in Wales. Another feature is the row of three freestanding stoves on the ground floor. These have Georgian Steel register grates that provide an almost traditional blackened texture combined with precise, polished stainless flues that run vertically through the space. The effect is far from minimalistic, while remaining faithful to the purity of the materials palette.

The overriding concept of jewels within a box permeates the two floors—with a continuing matrix of alternating transparent and translucent panels throughout the interior and exterior. This creates a tension between the dark joinery of a traditional British pub interior and the monochromatic blue and white Chinese ceramic tiling. The use of the flower motif is an ornamental adornment that complements the geometric patina of all the surfaces and is instrumental in providing the fusion between the two colliding aesthetics.

Created in collaboration with Yau's Turkish conceptual team Autoban, the upstairs dining room has stylish table settings spread across a series of banquettes and rectangular tables. Archer Humphryes enclosed the space within a horizontal band made from burnished steel with a wax finish— the architecture is carefully planned to allow the front facade to fully open so that the diners become part of the street performance within the market below.

A technical success, The Duck and Rice combines a state-of-the-art kitchen with a vocabulary of vibrant, dense pub activity to which Archer Humphryes has lent its creative flare and knowledge. Already, it has started a new trend of fusion pubs, beginning yet another chapter in the long and evolving pub story.

On the western side of the building, the architects worked with Westminster Planning Authority to successfully achieve a free-standing form as part of the regeneration of the protected Berwick Street market which has been in existence since the eighteenth century. By cantilevering the upper floor's concrete frame, more space becomes available for dining without taking away the pedestrian pathway at ground floor. External lights are reclaimed solid brass ship lights from Lassco salvage yard.

Sand-blasted forest brown marble forms the bar top surface on the ground floor; here the arrangement allows visibility to the street. The bar is an important part of the overall spatial arrangement—taking centre-stage on both ground and first floor.

Prominent in the design is the simplicity of the symmetrical concrete structure and the solidity of the mixed antique black handmade bricks by H Butterfield with black mortar. The 'trapezoidal' glass frontage is set back from the protruding frame of the building.

Round table tops in the same stone as the bar—forest brown—are arranged in an orderly way with the bench and stool seating, provided by De La Espada, forming the corner of the room. Their natural colours regress against the floral Chinese artistry of the traditional flattened blue and white pictorial motifs screen-printed onto white ceramic grid of tiles—an idea taken from simple kitchen pantries in Asia, and featured as decorative ideas in the architects' other restaurants Naamyaa and Aaya.

Here the trapezoidal pattern in a variety of views and different materials—illustrating how the architects have cleverly intertwined and woven the powerful geometry with the decoration of the architectural space: golden lily pads to the mirror frame; ribbed leather seating; veined marble relief; fine iron staircase from Brecon; icons for the male and female signage continuing a graphic language first developed in Busaba Eathai.

Circular globe wall lamps, redolent of
Kolo Moser's lamps from the turn of the
nineteenth century, were created by Autoban
for the project. Archer Humphryes' careful
positioning of them in the architecture
provides framed views through the screens.

Blue Corian forms the smooth basin with brass tap-ware. Here the floral pattern is intensified by also placing it on the ceiling, reflected in the mirror. Emperador marble for the floor, edged with flush bronze, completes the room. Oak doors and walls introduce a traditional Elizabethan tavern detail with expressed blackened screw heads evocative of traditional iron stable door hinges.

Descending to the basement, a wall of triangular mosaics in Cobalt Blue leads to the washrooms, with a frog's back bronze handrail to guide down the steps.

The circular staircase is a straightforward link between the bars at ground and first floor level. Bar seating curved against the facade frontage at the lower level frames the entranceway—a perfect overlooking point.

Copper tanks housing the unpasteurised beer for immediate consumption impact views at the entrance—making visible a segment of the art of brewing malted barley, yeast and water in its combined state. Their pure tubular perfection contrasts with the perforated filigree of the iron stair and the curved window facing the market.

A luxurious Spanish leather bar stool at a teardrop counter ledge overlooks the entrance—the perfect resting spot for a pint. Mimicking the ribbing of the seat is the beaded brass edge profile of the forest brown stone counter. The bronze rebated frame to the main facade window contrasts with the stripped concrete structural frame, which is a different order of architectural scale to the interior sections.

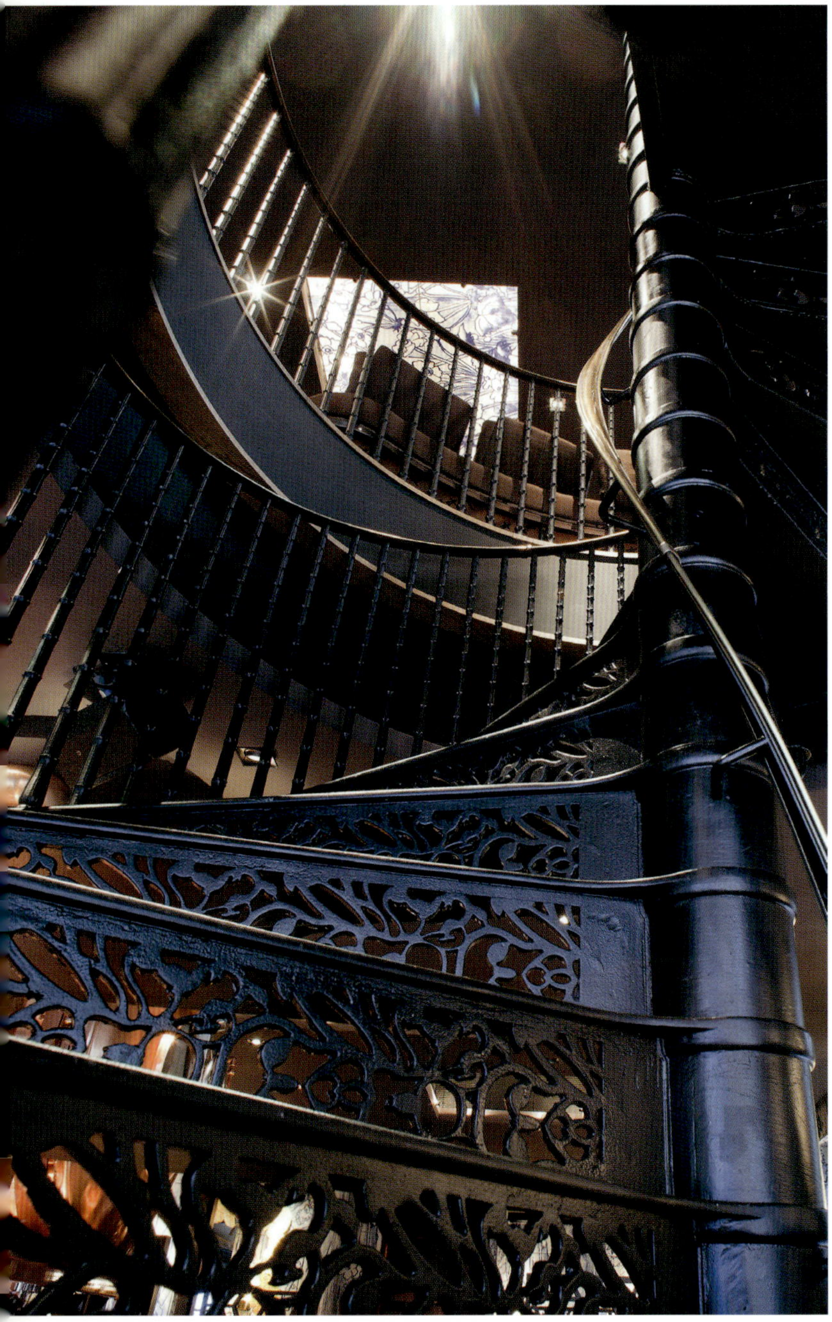
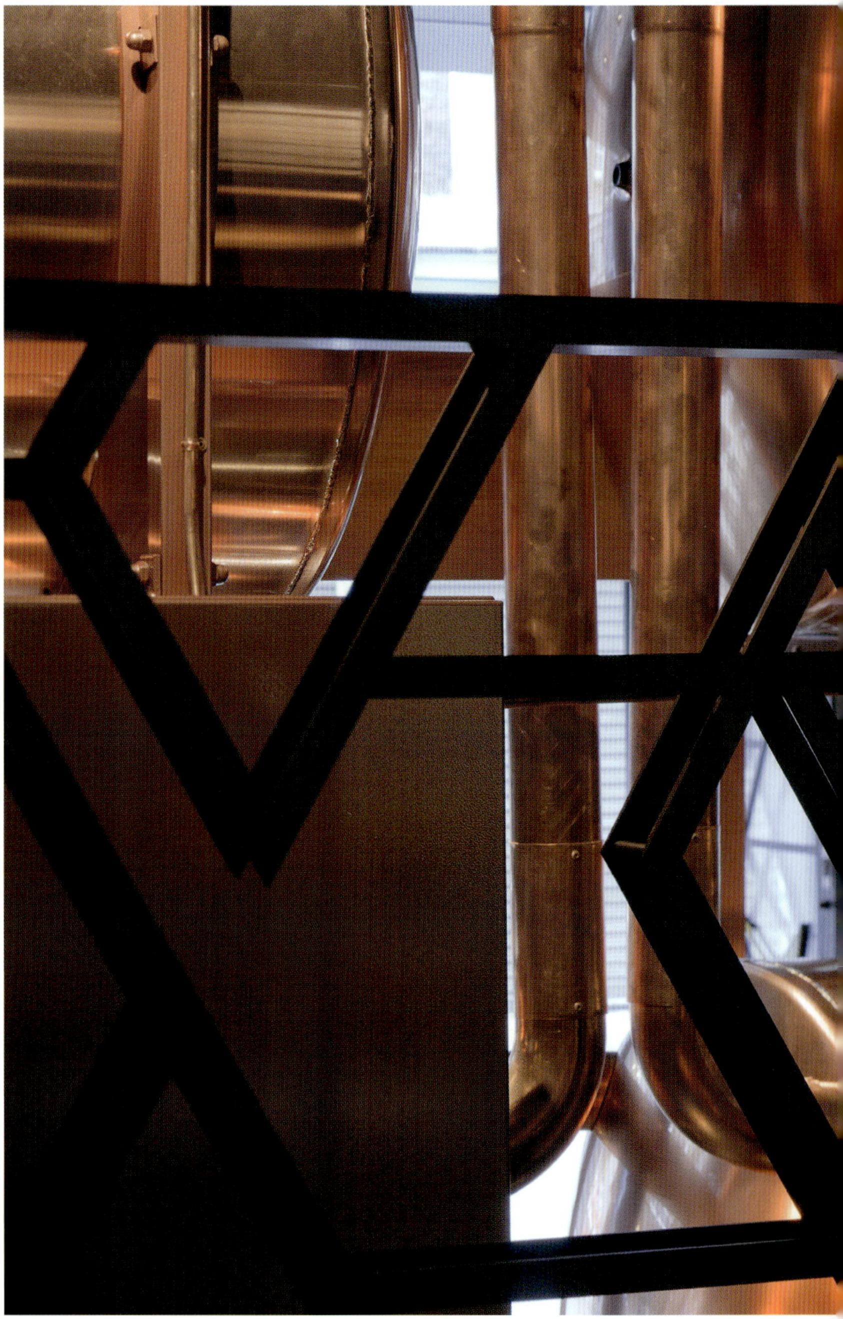

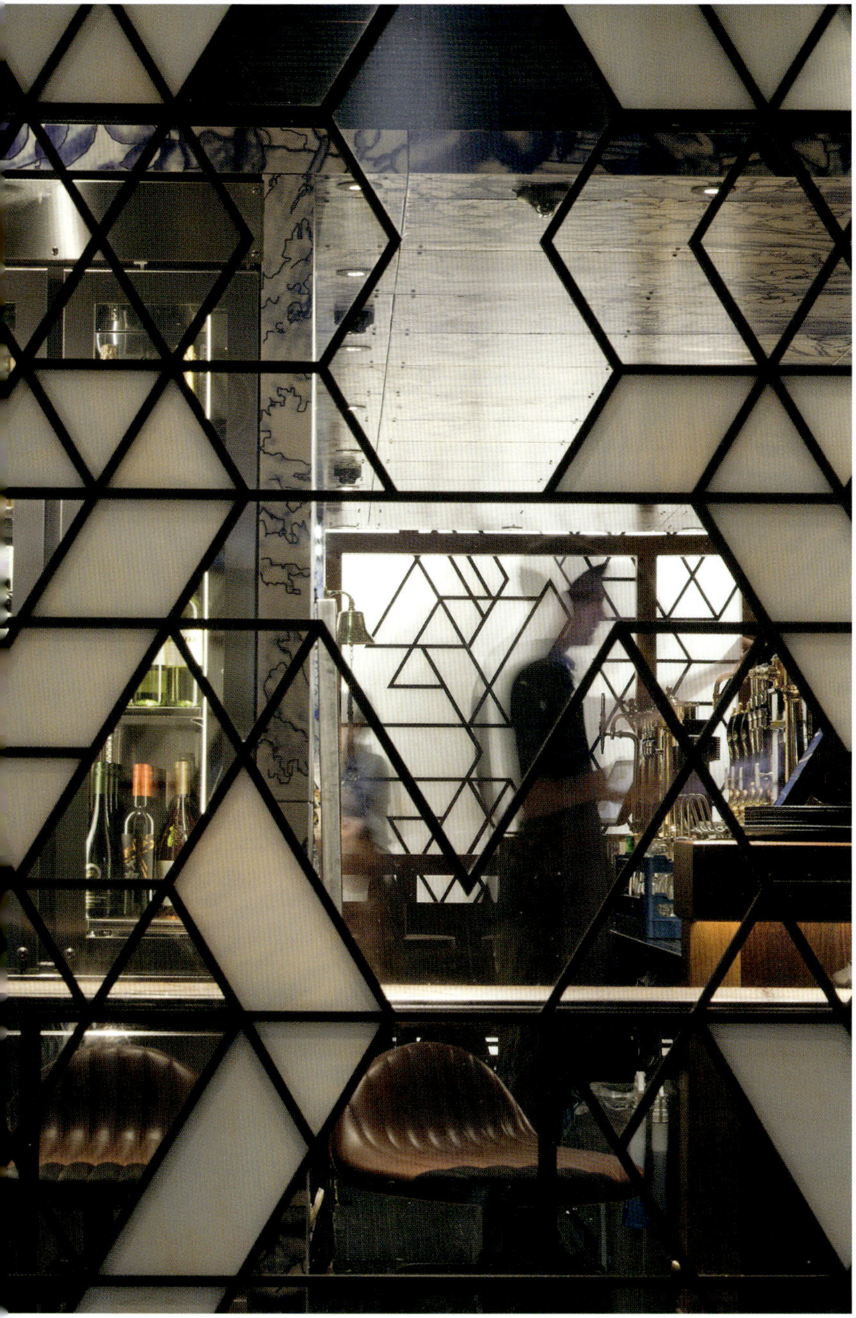

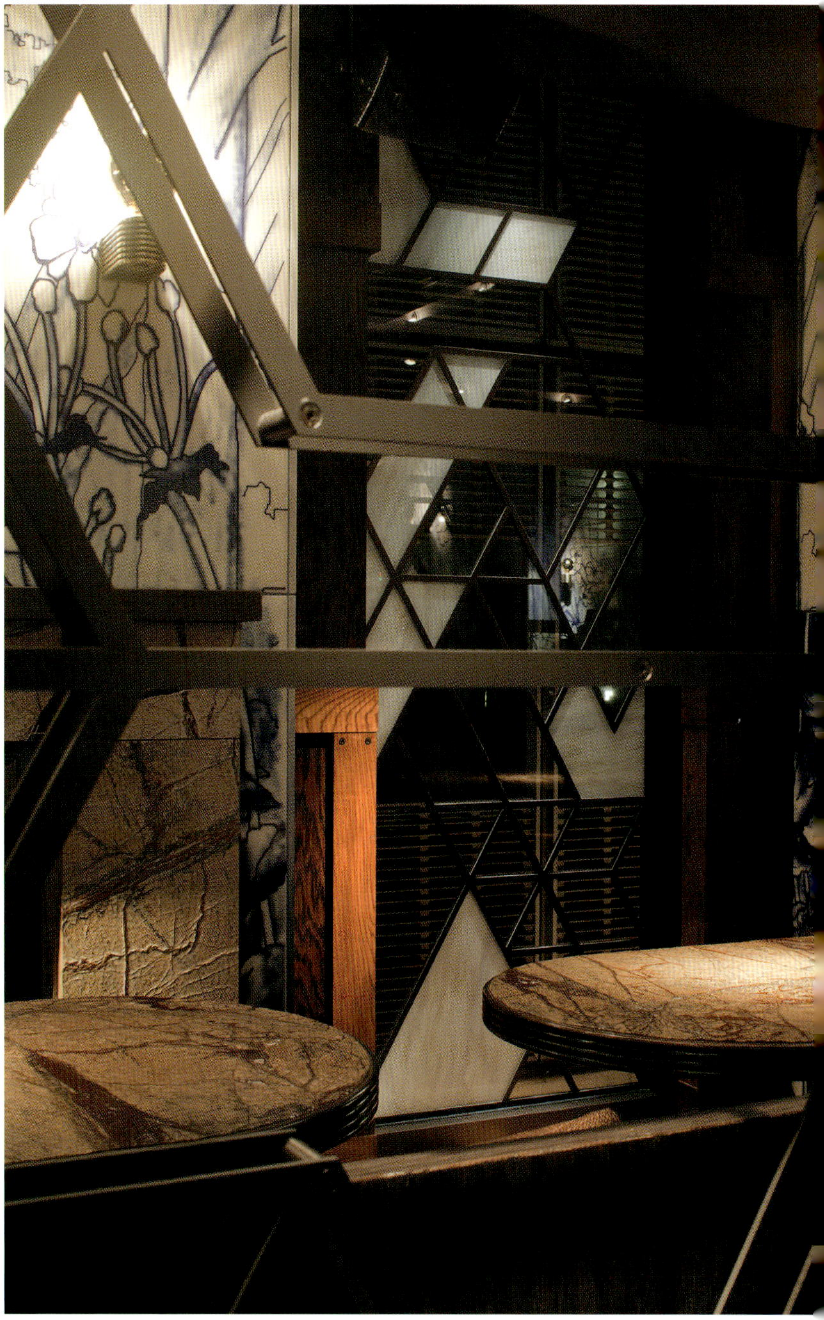

Three wood burning stoves on the ground floor create clusters of intimate seating for stools—providing warmth in winter, with the flame reflected in the highly-polished surfaces of the copper cylindrical tanks. Formed from Georgian steel register grate with bespoke sandblasted forest brown marble surrounds, the stoves stand out against the blue and white floral Chinese ceramics.

A back to a banquette is stitched together with bronze geometric Anolok screens—not dissimilar in intent to a traditional pew with a partition found in some public houses.

A Provintech wine dispenser unit from France, with state-of-the-art nitrogen preservation, is integrated into the back bar design. The architects have cleverly contained the chrome faucet bonnets within an aluminium-coated framework capable of multiple temperatures— carefully concealing the refrigeration of over 40 wine choices. Glowing opaline translucent glass emits from the backlit back bar.

A duck and drake together are a symbol of resourcefulness, fidelity, happiness and beauty in Chinese culture. The only overt acknowledgment to the name "Duck and Rice"—other than the pub sign on the front facade.

PRINT ROOM AND INK BAR

Occupying the former *Bournemouth Daily Echo* building, one of the most startling and dramatic buildings in the city, the Print Room and Ink Bar has transformed the 1934 Art Deco structure. The building was saved from a decade of decline, after the last newspaper rolled off the printing presses in 1994—a casualty of the inevitable decline in the use of the printing press in the new digital age.

In retaining not only the building but also the *Echo* signs, the clock jutting out over Richmond Hill and the name "The Print Room" for the exquisite dining space, this heroic architecture still exudes the confidence of its former proprietor, and the stark originality of the landmark, listed building by Seal and Hardy. This was a remarkable opportunity in an industrial space, to which Archer Humphryes responded by restoring the opulence seen in the building's former function—where the presses would have wheeled and thumped, pounding out Bournemouth's news day-by-day for 60 years—whilst today it pays homage to the grandeur described by others as: "A lavish classical space that's redolent of the drama of the era with its gleaming monochrome tiles, vast mirrors, maple wood panelled dining booths and spectacular, sparkling Swarovski crystal chandeliers."[29]

The result celebrates the mechanised modern world that the Art Deco designers of the past were preoccupied with and responds simultaneously to the human need for pleasure and escape through eating and conversation, celebrating these ephemeral qualities in the interior design. Evocative of the decadence of an F Scott Fitzgerald novel—with monochromatic abstraction of materials like a Rodchenko montage—the architects have at the same time been sympathetic to the building's historical setting. By radically adapting the architecture and interior, and by retaining the few surviving features, they have tantalisingly transformed the character of the building, allowing it to engage with the public, where previously it was a private space.

With the Print Room, Archer Humphryes has retained the seven-metre ceiling height and situated the restaurant in a generous open plan space, entered via retrofitted reeded glass double doors. Along one wall, the windows facing the street are above head height, while the very large windows along another face internal rooms—both retaining the original reed glass. Reeded glass is a recurrent theme in the architects' material palette; they first encountered its refractive translucent quality in the original plans for this project and have been introducing it consistently since. The material allows light to be distorted, creating an array of shadowy and contrasting forms.

After the volume of the space, lighting was the most significant technical consideration for the architects. The chandeliers create a dynamic activity of light through movement around the room, and it is the cut glass pendants and candle-lit lanterns that the designers created for the project that provide intimacy, paying homage to the formal dining booths of Chartier in Paris. Hovering delicately within the voluminous enclosure, the luminaires sit above high-backed banquette booths custom-built from oak to the architects' designs. Further ambient light is afforded via an array of LEDs that accentuate edges of window frames to refract red light along the vertical ribbed panels, thus introducing linear details into the monochromatic backdrop rather like a constructivist composition.

The overall lighting and seating arrangement is complemented by the less formal cafe, which is flanked by a patisserie and deli counter. The entire room is unified by the architects' introduction of black and white chequered terrazzo flooring, which adds a photographic abstraction to the room.

Located in the original reception room, the Ink Bar features dark stained bespoke tables and chairs that have coloured accents, with a specially selected 'peach colour', subsequently known as Farrow & Ball's 'Print Room Yellow'. This aesthetic continues in the *Echo* newspaper's former boardroom, which is now furnished with a grand black glass meeting table for private dining. Restored maple panelling is prominent in the interior detailing and cut glass decorative pendant lamps link the design back to the central space of the Print Room.

Whilst historical inventions such as the printing press change our urban environment, so new technological approaches eclipse what came before and make inventions redundant: the architectural challenge remains in creating new visual imagery whilst at the same time embracing the architectural order that remains. This is a privilege; the relationship between past, present and future is a difficult one to balance, and one that the architects have embraced in this project. This effort has been recognised in multiple awards and accolades. Going forwards, the digital age may change the way we think, shop, work or play in spaces. Its effect on desire and imagination—which still remain profound human experiences—is hard to disassemble.

"With the most primitive means the artist creates something which the most ingenious and efficient technology will never be able to create."[30]

In this voluminous restaurant of 400 square metres, the challenge was to refine an internal room without views to the outside and with an industrial height of seven metres, to seat 250, while simultaneously incorporating original Art Deco heritage into an ultra-modern brasserie setting. Chandeliers add elegance whilst scale and accents of red-edged lighting to the existing window frames, which used to overlook the newspaper presses, add piquancy and pizazz to the room.

Founded in 1900, in 1934 the *Bournemouth Daily Echo* began a glamorous era for the newspaper in a purpose-built Art Deco landmark. Using half a million bricks and large quantities of white Monks Park Bath stone, along with Purbeck stone in which discerning passers-by can still spot the fossils of shellfish from a million years ago, the "Echo" trademark is illuminated making it a beacon next to the Theatre in the centre of the city. With their careful interventions and modernisation, the architects' award-winning restaurant, which they appropriately named "The Print Room", reopened the space for the spectacular 1930s architecture to be celebrated.

Emblazoned transparent glass linear lanterns with cut bevelled flower ornamentation are modest details that compositionally create allure through the refractions of the light dancing around the space.

In The Print Room, the simplicity of a monochromatic palette of black and white table arrangements upon a chequered floor is electrified with glass lanterns and candlelight. As is customary in the practice's work, all the decorative pendants are designed by Archer Humphryes and manufactured by Jonathan Coles for the project.

Eye level intimacy in this tall room is achieved where lanterns are suspended above the 'carriage-style' seating, whilst the chandeliers are infinitely reflected at high level by a mirror, meticulously positioned to create a redolent grandeur.

A pewter bar runs the length of the room, with bottle displays arranged in grand cabinets following the window arrangement overhead. Top-lit with natural daylight, the orthogonal ordering of the dining achieves a solid, rigorous and regular expression to this airy former machine room.

Poured terrazzo and the decorative
use of a wrought iron balustrade
flows into the appropriately named
"The Ink Bar".

Flashes of yellow, taken from the face of the Art
Deco clock found in what used to be the newsroom,
appears subtly in the furniture design and in 'off
stage' spaces, framed by dark Wenge openings.

PEYTON AND BYRNE

Described by Matthew Fort as having a "penchant for the spectacular and the idiosyncratic", Oliver Peyton is a renowned restaurateur and the founder and chairman of Peyton and Byrne, a company known for its impressive restaurant designs.[31] Bringing Marc Newson's feverishly adventurous new dining experience which looks to the future rather than the past to Mayfair in the 1990s in Coast, defined Peyton as a London restaurateur brimming with ideas. Having visited Aaya in Soho in 2008, he contacted Archer Humphryes as he was expanding his chain of Peyton and Byrne bakeries across London. Included in this was the stand-alone bakery-cafe in the entrance of Renzo Piano's St Giles Circus, near Covent Garden, for which he initially secured the architects' assistance, leading to a subsequent multi-project developmental collaboration. The bakeries offer a "quintessentially British experience" presenting pretty pastel-coloured shops stacked with freshly made breads, English sponges and puddings.

Manifestly a lobby experience, the location of the bakery was within a building that has been described by critics as Piano's "wilfully vivid" development.[32] "Reaching out to its context at the same time as boldly asserting its own personality", the bakery absorbs the street scene through the central courtyard, establishing physical and visual links to its surroundings.[33] Orange terracotta tiles, in their tens of thousands, are highly visible through the layers of glass and metal skin, drawing you straight to the counter of the bakery.

Inserting a rustic bakery into a dominant high rise is not a new concept for monetising and mobilising a 'lobby experience'; it trades like a traditional covered market square in the community. The concept follows the same principles governed by a large master-planning project: attention to the location and geography of the position, applying logic to the order of activities of the space and understanding the content. Experience of the 'lobby' from private space to public space, to the static space of the building and the 'performance' of the occupants are all interchanges in a 'fluid' space within which only the architecture retains its permanence.

Piano is known for stating: "Architecture is art, architecture is many, many things. Architecture is science, is technology, is geography, is typography, is anthropology, is sociology, is art, is history. You know all this comes together. And, by the way, architecture is also a very polluted art in the sense that it's polluted by life, and by the complexity of things."[34]

The orange wall provided by Piano's building acts as a beacon to passersby, enticing them in. Once inside, the bakery has the opportunity to become the epicentre, where a visitor can hold a quick meeting, grab a drink and a bite to eat, or gather in a casual social setting to do some work as a break out from office culture. This new direction of multi-function and flexibility is derived directly from the needs and wants of the community and not solely from the design, which provides the platform for opportunity.

A very straightforward proposition was taken forward, orthogonal in plan, and reacting within its envelope, in order to be given prominence in the lobby 'experience' and become a commercially visible success. In stark contrast to Piano's architecture, the servery is a block of Carrera white marble, inset with a hot plate in pure white Kashmir granite. Behind the servery, the walls are detailed in 'ice white' Corian. The pastel colours of the Peyton and Byrne products are punched out against the back wall through the graphic design, "a cohesive programme of meticulous detail that can be applied to many products uniquely and manage to make a simple box of treats feel like a box of jewels".[35] The design intends to simplify, not to add to the complexity and confusion within the lobby.

Further colour punctuation is lent to the space by the layout of the bright red mesh Alias chairs and the mezzanine, which slides against the orange terracotta appliqué wall.

Colour in this project enters the collective consciousness of the community; no one can escape the orange, lemon and lime corpus, or prepare you for it. The bakery that Archer Humphryes has created presents a cool counterpoint to the explosion of potent kaleidoscopic colour. Italian architect Renzo Piano explains: "I wanted to make a building that smiles"—and in turn the architects wanted to make a bakery that you can dream in.[36]

At ground floor the cafe space is conceived to be as transparent as possible with a six metre-high, fully-glazed window facade which gives views of the courtyard with an oak tree at its heart, emphasising the permeability of the site, and making Peyton and Byrne visible to the outside. Red chairs harmonise with the strong oranges and distinguish the cafe from the surrounding office environment. Red is matched exactly with the mezzanine handrail pantone, connecting the cafe vertically and defining the boundary in the open lobby.

A mezzanine for casual seating sits above the main cafe. Here the leather upholstery is a simple stone colour against the bright orange ceramic wall, which is the dominant feature in the building. Reflections upon the 'low iron' glass balustrade create the enclosure to the seating.

SAVERNAKE HOTEL AND RESORT

An astonishing grand avenue of beech trees forms a processional route to Tottenham House and Park from the forest of Savernake, which disorientates the traveller along the Saddle Ride via focused views, passing veteran trees, the oldest in Europe. And yet few are aware that what characterises Savernake most are the remnants of an eighteenth-century landscape laid out by two of the most influential figures of the period: Lord Burlington and Lancelot "Capability" Brown.

When Archer Humphryes first made the approach to Tottenham House along the avenue, they sensed the illusion created by the eighteenth-century landscape vista design, despite the slow decay of this once magnificent Palladian country house. On that crisp winter morning, they stood in the stable block, which was fit for 40 horses and six carriages, with workers' quarters in the rooms above. Two pure white barn owls appeared, at first almost motionless, before quickly flying into a conifer plantation.

The Grade I listed Regency house—constructed in Bath stone, and with more than 100 rooms and a stable block—had been leased by the Earl of Cardigan and Viscount Savernake to Buena Vista who, via a collaboration with English Heritage, had received planning permission to save Tottenham House from dereliction. Originally built in 1820 under the first Marquess of Ailesbury, by Thomas Cundy the Elder, it incorporates parts of earlier houses on the site, including Lord Burlington's house design from 1721.

It was a once-in-a-lifetime commission for the architects to work with the team that Buena Vista had assembled. The remit was largely based around remodelling and preserving whilst, at the same time, adding imaginative architectural design in order to revive the splendour that remains throughout the House and Park, reinvigorating it as the Savernake Club, Spa and Golf Resort—an array of disciplines that required a simple organisation of principles before drawing. The brief was vast. The main house has incredible intact interiors: the music room features exquisite marquetry floors, Italian pilaster work and monumental ceilings in an eighteenth-century Empire style; the Prince Regent bath—owing its name to the famous guest—is carved from Statuario marble; an Orangery, whose glass was destroyed by a nearby bomb blast in the Second World War, when the Americans stayed in the house to prepare for D-Day; and the Rotunda, with its coffered ceiling and oculus used as a private chapel. Carefully reorganising the principal rooms, the architects returned its status to that of a resplendent residence with a new purpose: a hotel. Utilising all of their creative and technical ability to inform and develop the luxury architecture, interiors and grounds in a historic setting, by restoring and upgrading it to a stupendous landmark and a destination hotel was the aim of the task. The architects created 17 suites in the main house with the use of antiques and delectably designed furniture purpose made for the house, and accessories and art carefully selected to complement the overall vision and atmosphere: a perfect ambience in which club members and guests could enjoy the many restaurants, bars and lounges, not to mention the world-class spa in the stable block, with a generous glass-covered pool in the courtyard. Outdoor pursuits are arranged in the adjacent buildings—all architectural gems reached through new walkways introduced into the listed landscape and factored in to the extensive space required for golfing visitors. The necessary views of the Italian Parterre, 'pleasure gardens', sunken lawns and woodlands originally conceived by Lord Burlington and Lancelot Brown were opportunities for the architects to introduce interventions into the landscape, enticing the prospective guest into its historical legacy.

Portraits which tell the story of the life of the house line the atrium of the grand staircase. The house has been made particularly famous by its illustrious personage, especially Jane Seymour—whose father was the forest steward and to whom Henry VIII proposed in the ancient forest—and the seventh Earl, who led the Charge of the Light Brigade against the Russian guns at Balaclava during the Crimean War. Over 31 generations of ownership and 1,000 years, it has never once been bought or sold, and today it is the only ancient forest in Britain still in private hands.

There is a clear understanding in Archer Humphryes' work on the project that the house's future depends on an enrichment of what exists, rather than imitating an artificial folly that is devoid of any connection to its origins. Finding an architectural language that links the old and new in an overwhelmingly *current* morphosis is an analytical process that suspends the plasticity of the form, with its underlying purpose and unchangeable merits—an activity the architects perpetually elicit.

Bombed during the D-day campaign, when the house was commandeered by the American Armed Forces, the conservatory constructed from wrought iron vaulted structure, seen from the air, links to the Orangerie where it opens directly into an Italian-inspired *parterre* garden. Tottenham House is the centrepiece of the Savernake Estate which, for 31 generations, has continued in legacy, starting with Lord Cardigan's ancestor, a knight who fought alongside William the Conqueror. Responding to the immense task of returning the property to a resplendent luxury hotel, the architects redefined the 5,000 acres of forest and parkland, returning the House to its former glory in the estate.

Remnants of the original eighteenth-century landscape laid out by Lancelot "Capability" Brown can be seen along the driveway, which has beech trees planted in an arrangement that is said to be derived from cavalry battalion formations, connecting the Grade I listed house to the ancient forest. The core of the house was created by Lord Burlington, crescent wings being added by the architect Henry Flitcroft and further enlargement by Thomas Cundy, beginning in 1823, where previously, in 1818 he had designed the stables for the Marquess of Ailesbury. Natural woodland is interwoven with modern conifer plantation and impressive specimen trees, including an imported Redwood from California, resulting in a pleasure garden with an equal listing to the house.

In the process of generating the design to reinstate the magnificence of the Palladian stately home into a new hotel, a technical survey of photographs and drawings was recorded by Archer Humphryes, and relied upon to generate thinking to the newly defined sequence of principal rooms, which includes: the Music Room with its intricate marquetry floor, the Atrium Staircase, with its lantern skylight, the Library with solid carved statuesque marble fireplaces and the Rotunda chapel with its incredible plaster coffers and oculus.

Famous owners are part of the frescos that are painted directly onto the dry lime plaster following the tradition of the Italian Renaissance. Lord Cardigan, famed for his epic failure of the Light Brigade, features in the paintings along the great staircase, and of whom was said: "After riding back up the valley, he considered he had done all that he could and then, with considerable sang-froid, left the field and went on board his yacht in Balaclava harbour, where he ate a champagne dinner."

LALIT HOTEL LONDON

Archer Humphryes' extensive redevelopment of Edward Mountford's 1893 St Olave's Grammar School was the first of the practice's projects with Berkeley Homes to obtain planning permission. The address of One Tower Bridge—nestled against the Lord Mayor's building and overlooking the Thames, the Tower of London and Tower Bridge to the north—is an impressive one.

Berkeley Homes sold the property to Dr Jyotsna Suri, the widow of Lalit Suri, thus initiating the second assignment on the site for the architects; this time transposing the interior into a vivid hotel, to be completed as part of Lalit's legacy, by his family and in his honour: "An entrepreneur, a politician, an avid art collector and a philanthropist. Lalit Suri, Chairman and Managing Director of Bharat Hotels, was a respected figure in domestic and international community for his vision and dynamism. If he was better known for his achievements as a hotelier, he also made his share of contribution in the Indian political system as a sitting Member of Parliament."[37] Originating from the rail-town of Rawalpindi in Pakistan, Lalit moved to Delhi and subsequently built an extensive hotel empire. He sadly, and suddenly, died in London at the age of 59. He left to his wife his wish to create a sublime hotel residence in the heart of his favourite city.

Jyotsna—known for her "vociferous promotion of Indian Tourism, an art patron and the chairperson of one of India's fastest growing hotel groups"—was keen for Archer Humphryes to sensitively respect the intrinsic quality of Mountford's architectural design whilst incorporating an Indian cultural identity in the fabric of the interior as a conceptual necessity.[38] Typical details of 'Edwardian Baroque architecture' include extensive 'rustication' and exaggeration of the 'voissours' of arched openings at the ground floor, both of which form part of the landmark building's civic heritage. Integrating the patently Indian themes within the existing language of the building had precedents. The 'Grand Style' during the British Empire that Sir Edward Lutyens exported when he created the official residence for the Viceroy of India—"Rashtrapati Bhavan" a 'city' becoming known as the 'Delhi Order' in Jyotsna's home city—encapsulates this. Formed of red sandstone, its Mughal scale reflects the Red Fort in New Delhi—from where the British Indian Government exiled the then emperor in 1857—manifesting itself as an 'imperialistic' architecture.

After visiting the Red Fort, the architects decided to examine the Indian cultural themes of the past. The ornamental work in the residence—a synthesis of Persian, Indian and European with extensive expressive colour—was immediately absorbing. An 'imitation of paradise' the garden complex of the Red Fort historically contained a piece of furniture called the Peacock Throne. The legend of this throne visually informed the architects as to the richness and opulence of historic Indian structures, factors subsequently reflected in the architectural embellishment. The buildings emerged as symbols of 'lavish luxury' that the former emperors entwined with Imperialist rule; not dissimilar to the origins of Mountford's aesthetic in genesis, though the cultural backgrounds in which they were embedded were inexorably unconnected, the Red Fort being a symbol of power and Mountford's school a place for social exchange of knowledge.

By keeping the original 'Edwardian Baroque' details within the 70 room hotel, but adding decoration and embellishment in traditional Indian furniture and antiques, sourced by the architects in Delhi, a harmonious Indian-Anglo aesthetic ignites the interior design of the stupendous halls and rooms of the project. Exotic mother of pearl inlaid as encrusted gems into furniture reliefs, applique silk tapestries, and huge Hyderabad chandeliers, shimmering like diamonds in the sky, are some of the delights that greet the visitor, against a backdrop of existing white rococo pilaster ceiling work. A peacock tapestry—reminiscent of the aforementioned golden Peacock Throne—forms part of the bedhead in every room. In 1655 the French jeweller Tavernier described the spectacle as a bed—a *takhteh*—when he saw the Koh-I-Noor diamond and the Timur Ruby encrusted in the throne, before it disappeared after the Emperor's assassination, never to reappear.[39] The Koh-I-Noor is permanently displayed at the Tower of London, a stone's throw from the hotel across the Thames. Having been a resident at the Tower in her 20s, Humphryes often observed its radiance; the diamond was confiscated from the Sikh empire and passed to the Empress of India in 1877, Queen Victoria, before being set within the crown of Queen Elizabeth II.

As initially stated in a Hindu text of 1306: "He who owns this diamond will own the world, but will also know all its misfortunes. Only God, or a woman, can wear it with impunity."[40]

Representing Autumn, the Peacock Gate at the Chandra Mahal in the Jaipur City Palace, Rajasthan, has a kaleidoscope of colours: deep cerulean blue, yellow ochre and burnt sienna, which are the key tones for the design of the new hotel.

In the former Assembly Hall of the grammar school, the hotel's restaurant has Hyderbad chandeliers suspended in the vault where blue is deployed as the primary decoration with golden stars hand-painted onto the plasterwork, a pietra dura. Every surface has been redefined by the architects, creating a chamber of bejewelled refinement, table tops of mother of pearl, sedan seating with delicate carvings and jali screens.

In each bedroom a tapestry damask silk applique 'rangoli' depicts two symmetrical peacocks, framed to sit above ornate carved beds. Following on from long traditions of folk art, the bedhead idea was borne out of the architects trip to India, and the client's wish that a distinct Indo-Anglo direction be interwoven thematically into the artistry of the hotel. In generating the pictorial work, repeating geometric forms and natural life-forms found in the ornamentation of Lal Qila steered the architectural thinking for screens, surfaces and textiles throughout the hotel.

Lutyens' Viceroy's palace, now known as Rashtrapati Bhavan in New Delhi, dominates the graded avenue approach with its massive scale is mitigated by the surrounding English and Moghul gardens. On a visit to New Delhi its presence cannot be negated. Indo-Anglo architecture, it was constructed from the same cultural background as Edward Mountford's modest St Olave's School in London.

Upon visiting the Diwan-i-Aam in Delhi, the powerful colour of the red, found in the sandstone arcades with nine engraved arch openings, resonated as a primary base for the canvas of the projects palette, which the joinery in the scheme picks up. Lord Curzon restored the Hall of Audience with the Florentine artist, Mennegatti where ornamentation with gilded gold and white shell lime chunam plaster work is now almost lost once more on the stones surface.

A corridor of red sandstone found at the mosque on the western side of the Taj Mahal forms a perspectival vista with the arcades fronting the gardens. Famous for the architectural garden complex that is symmetrically composed, only five gardens remain in Agra. The design was conceived as both an earthly replica of the house of Mumtaz in paradise and an instrument of propaganda for the Moghul emperor who created the site initially.

The intricate inlay, carving and incised painting of the Taj Mahal ceiling is a clear example of integration of traditional Persian and Hindu decorative elements where abstract geometric patterns can be described as 'lapidary'. Throughout the project the architects remind the hotel guests of initial visit to India and its importance to the scheme generation in their modern application. In the Clerks' Bar, a ceiling made entirely of black and white mother of pearl will be the defining element of the room.

In the Governors' bar, octagonal pearlescent tables and banquettes in corresponding shapes will be beautifully appointed to be symmetrical on axis with the existing ornate stone fireplace. Cherubs in the pilaster carved ceiling reveal the heritage of the interior and will still preside over the room's new venue.

Here a garden terrace will be introduced against the tall windows of the restaurant in front of the existing Edwardian Baroque facade where the architects will distinguish the clock tower by dramatic lighting, creating a new hotspot in this fashionable area of London Bridge Quarter next to Tower Bridge.

Details of existing American walnut "oak panelled" walls, carved stone arches, iron trusses of the vaulted ceiling and the gallery above the Assembly Hall, which will become spaces for afternoon tea and the restaurant, respectively.

COURT ESSINGTON

A magnificent Arts and Crafts property dating from 1903, Court Essington embodied the symbolism of its origins at the cusp of modernity; its incredible setting was an inspiration to Archer Humphryes. Set below Midford Castle and commanding panoramic views across the Frome Valley towards Norton Saint Philips and beyond, framed by rolling green hills, fragrant with freshly mowed grass, it is surrounded by a world that has inspired many poets—William Wordsworth marked the beginning of the Romantic movement with his work in Somerset.

Here was a place that had picture-perfect vistas and a long provenance of artists seeking meaning in the sublimity of the natural landscape and light. The outdoor setting defines the approach taken by the architects to the interior and the building.

A family intimately involved in the music industry, with whom the architects had been engaged on a number of discrete projects previously, wanted to create a home for a modern family in Somerset: remodelling, restoring and renovating the house and preserving its essential features followed. Country houses are part of the rural psyche in England with Court Essington being no exception. The property was in decline at the point of commission; on arrival as guests for the weekend, the architects imagined a past world of servants and grandeur, which could have been woven into a Henry James novel. Full of optimism, they set about the enormous task of translating an old archaic masterpiece into a modern family home.

In response to the landscape, they opened up the Edwardian house plan to provide spacious interiors with framed views and capturing light in every room. In a way, the country home with its past adherence to social and economic Edwardian etiquette, was edited by the remodelling, making way for an architectural order that no longer had the constraints of an antiquated class society. Instead the ideals and materials for the home represented simplicity, arranged as a succession of spaces completely re-planned in relation to key vistas and openings, beginning with the gardens. Terracing and stepped gardens are connected by walkways with fragrant meadow flowers that the architects planned and ordered in the landscape, while a new pool is a testament to stone wall construction by local Somerset master craftsmen. The erudite personality of the owner is reflected in the entire project and the pool is a perfect backdrop for family gatherings, where guests can sit playing music whilst breathing in the aromatic scent of fresh-planted mint and rosemary.

Beginning with the main house, the architects created a spectacular conservatory formed from stone and glass, positioned prominently on a new garden terrace offering vistas across the estate. The conservatory forms the first space where the process of rethinking the placing of every door and window in the new buildings to create striking perspectives of the landscape setting started.

Reached from the conservatory, the kitchen is best described as a 'creamery'. With an Aga, a homework table for the children, the cooking utensils arranged above, the feeling is very rural. Both the conservatory and the creamery have a palette of warm whites which reflect and absorb the sunshine.

A large manor house, it has a Great Hall, with an open fire, to brighten British winters. Moving deeper into the plan of the house, the colour palette intensifies, with gold decorative wall paper lining corridors, yellow ochre in the pantry, 'card room green' in the library, a polka dot wall paper in the guest room and a violent red in the Great Hall, which absorbs the glow of firelight.

Upstairs, master bedroom and bathroom are located on the south side of the house where light bathes the walls throughout the day. Panelled and painted with *eau de Nile*, and punctuated by the 'framed view openings', the geometric panelling adds structure to the interior spaces. In the tranquil private bathroom, white slab marble lines the room. A freestanding roll top bath is introduced as a romantic reminiscence of the project's Edwardian origins. Mirrors above the voluptuous console have been placed to reflect the Arcadian Somerset countryside and the sunshine blazes in dramatically, creating warmth. Children's bedrooms have fireplaces and all the magical enchantments of bunk beds, rumpus rooms and secret fairy-tale hiding spaces.

As a finishing touch, Archer Humphryes added antiques. Metal Moroccan lanterns and objects from afar with patterns inspired by the English countryside emphasise the quality of the materials used as a hint to the beginnings of the architectural routes of this building at the eve of the twentieth century.

Immaculately restored, here the manor house was remodelled with the introduction of a conservatory, stepped landscape and impressive leaded windows invoking the original character of the Arts and Crafts house, which commands impressive vistas across the vale of Somerset.

Entrances to the principal bedrooms have been reorganised to give definition to the window framing the landscape view and to provide additional accommodation for a large family.

In the hallway, the new staircase and simple panels to the wall, both in eggshell, add a domestic appeal to the grand house, where a myriad of golden bumblebees are hand painted onto wallpaper. Originally found in Josephine Bonaparte's bedchamber in silk, the bumblebees provide a graphic repetition which is mirrored in the upper landing.

In the master bathroom, a pedestal console, La Chapelle, was specially commissioned as a double with two corresponding beveled mirrors reflecting the tranquil lush landscape of the surrounding six-acre estate.

A children's bathroom is crisp and cool in pure white surfaces. Purely conveying a practical rustic environment, a roll-top bath, centred on the doorway and timber v-jointing connecting the walls and ceiling, complete the room.

After visiting Mellerstain House, a stately home in the Scottish Borders, where a creamery barn sits in a vernacular cobbled courtyard holding the dairy herds before processing the milk, the architects likened the elementariness of this rural activity to how a country house should feel. It was the basis for the design development for the kitchen in particular, with rudimentary white porcelain tiles, granite surfaces and painted doors.

A contemporary satin-finished metal lantern is discrete above the doorway enveloped with foliage, with a new wide entrance door placed in the porch, naturally pinched in the pivot point of two wings of the house, recreating the Arts and Craft feel effortlessly.

In the main reception room, a double-height, barrel-vaulted ceiling with the fireplace at its heart, is accented with a 'rectory red' wall which is mirrored on the facing wall with a cathedral style window looking onto the gardens.

Delicate steel trusses are painted to match the stone green of the window frames and the masonry structure leading to the pool in the garden. Conceived as a symmetrical room that harmonises with the Bath stone facade, its proportion and material content was carefully considered to enhance the house.

A coach house in the grounds was rebuilt to create guest accommodation. A solid oak structure, sensitively cantilevered off the amended floor slab, illustrates an important constraint of the brief, which emphasised the view of the surrounding countryside by widening the angle from the interior, achieved by the depth and breadth of the new facade.

BUXTON CRESCENT HOTEL

AND GAINSBOROUGH HOTEL

Work to restore and develop both Buxton Crescent and the Gainsborough Hotel in Bath with the Osborne Property Group began Archer Humphryes long-term association with this client and deep connections with the respective cities. Trevor Osborne has been instrumental in the evolution of the practice, providing many initial important projects.

Buxton and Bath follow the tradition of spa towns, with thermal baths from mineral hot springs as the main component for the sites, using the pure extracted water reputed since Victorian times to have healing qualities. The architects planned complex treatment suites in the hotels and, with their knowledge of emerging spas across the world, were able to be informative, directing the client with imaginative ideas on the use of water in the hotel, with a rational ordered approach to redefining the place today. A long lineage of visitors seeking recuperation and relaxation in the cities meant the architects' proposal should not detract from the origins of the place.

Restoring the redundant crescent building in the centre of Buxton to its former glory and attaching it to the oldest hotel still in existence in Britain was the starting point. In Buxton, the settlement was first known to Romans as *Aquae Arnemetiae*, or the "spa of the goddess of the grove". A combination of complex masterplanning, complicated Heritage funding, extraction rights with Perrier and dealings with local councillors in the Peak District who were immensely persistent about the potential of the location meant that finally, after a decade, work to breathe life into the noble city had begun. Re-establishing its importance has enabled the architects to link the site to Joseph Paxton's Opera House and Spring Gardens from 1840, providing a new public square to the west of the Crescent which physically connects to the historic centre of Buxton with its commercial district, and provides ten retail units opening onto the Colonnade. A Grade I listed masterpiece from 1780 by John Carr of York is conserved, along with the adjacent pump room and external areas. In the interiors, the creation of a ballroom, an outdoor pool, a dance studio and exercise area support the vast suite of treatment spaces; the 90-room hotel was arranged. The practice's initial work on the city masterplan to reinstate the historical site in the public realm will be felt by the residents for years to come. It has been a triumph for the city made only possible by the geographic constraints of the Crescent's position and the architects' pragmatic response to the brief's content.

The city of Bath equally has been an enduring 'wellness' destination for over 2,000 years. Bath was first recorded as a shrine to "Sulis", a Celtic mother goddess. Its thermal waters, naturally permeating, were encircled within a large Roman settlement, which adopted "Sulis" within its temples, today enshrined within one of the city's finest hotels, the Gainsborough Bath Spa.

From the 1820s, John Pinch's design for The Gainsborough (renamed later after Sir Thomas Gainsborough, the famed Victorian society portrait and landscape artist who lived and worked in Bath) began as the United Hospital where thermal waters were used medicinally. Excavation in 1864 revealed several rooms belonging to an ancient complex that included the remains of an intricate Roman mosaic dating back to the fourth century. Remaining preserved, it sits beneath as an exact replica within the spa. In 2007 a Roman hoard of 17,500 coins was discovered amongst the foundations. Now with the British Museum, the hoard dates from 32 BC to 270 AD and is amongst the largest coin hoards yet discovered in Britain.

Demands upon this landmark site were technically onerous. A commission to extract water for the spa without disturbing the equilibrium of the subterranean Roman complex was something the architects had become experts at through the association with Buxton and the client. Set in the heart of this historic city, The Gainsborough Bath Spa is a collection of three listed buildings: The Gainsborough and Bellotts each distinguished by their Georgian facades and Hetling House, an Elizabethan building.

The project began with sensitive restoration, connection to adjacent properties and new designs for additions to the historic premises to create a viable hotel. The desire of the client was a state of the art interior to meet the expectations of the discerning luxury lifestyle industry while remaining authentic to its context in Bath. Producing a subtle architecture, which sits harmoniously within the historic fabric of a heritage site, was foremost in the architects' minds and the city's. The new detached building alongside the old re-formed architecture, creating 100 rooms met with the approval of English Heritage. A spa pool within an atrium of a new glazed courtyard is the dramatic centrepiece that unites the old and new, framing the city through the windows as the backdrop to the serenity of the spa.

Snow fall in the Peak District, a route
regularly taken from London to Buxton
in the heart of Derbyshire. "The town's
rich history features Roman settlers, royal
prisoners, outlaws and noble benefactors."

Georgian Crescent, a luxury spa hotel, was part of the architects' masterplan to re-engage the civic centre with its historic past. A complicated, successful planning application, connecting the building to the Paxton gardens and extracting Buxton spring water for the spa programme, includes extending the building dramatically to house a glass pool with panoramic of the crescent and an arcade for retail, reinvigorating the town.

A new architecture wing at the Gainsborough Bath Spa Hotel is the latest addition to a collection of three listed buildings, including Bellotts, which the architects sensitively stitched together forming a grand hotel in a Unesco city. Synonymous with a city whose history is infused with Roman baths, the design included three pools and direct access to the natural thermal waters adjacent to the ancient monuments, for which the practice successfully achieved planning consent.

Royal Circus, by John Wood, was considered a masterpiece of his career and its urban relationship with the Bath Abbey, the Roman Baths and the Gainsborough are what make up the urban plan of the city. This relationship cannot fail to influence design, and Archer Humphryes have been fortunate to complete many projects in the environs of this ancient place, which is only understood by walking through it.

AMANZI TEA

A Zulu word for water, *amanzi,* was a natural way to tie the Southern African heritage of the company's Zimbabwean owners to the core element used in brewing tea. In a few short years, Amanzi Tea has experienced exponential growth. The idea started with a pilot cart in Miami in 2006; an explosive response resulted in the first international store. Bringing Amanzi Tea from America to London was owner Levy's dream, cementing the company's reputation, tea being the most consumed drink after water. Essentially a tea bar and retail store, representing the flagship for the business, the concept that the client asked Archer Humphryes to develop was a prototype for a "projected chain of characterful tea shops".

The brief to the designers described the product as a combination of classic blends with luscious flavours, that follow a heritage of world tea cultivation, known for its powerful antioxidants. Tea culture has a long history as part of oriental ceremonies and ritualised protocols associated with meditation, becoming popular in British culture in the seventeenth century— which is why the choice of the city was important in the company's venture.

In Japan, the tea ceremony developed into a 'metamorphic practice' allowing the participants to transform themselves; an aesthetic behaviour was created from the rituals of *sabis* and *wabis* principles. The architects' familiarity with the concept of opposites—the inner spiritual and outer material side of life—helped in resolving how to represent in the same space tea in its raw imperfect state alongside the activity of tasting the refined tea. Emptiness, in Japanese custom, was considered the most effective means to spiritual awakening, while "embracing imperfection was honoured as a healthy reminder to cherish our unpolished selves, here and now, just as we are—the first step to 'satori' or enlightenment."[41] The rich in Britain imported the Japanese custom as part of their cargo: porcelain tea pots, tea bowls and neat little jars for storing the tea came too until, over time, differing cultural patterns emerged leading to the kitsch perception of quaint afternoon tea. The floral design of Amanzi's products and packaging take on the handpainted quality of the figurative calligraphic lines of traditional pure oriental porcelains, long associated with Western interpretation of the activity of sipping tea from ornamental objects: the cup and saucer. The architectural design drew upon ideas from every element of the client's initial 'pilot cart' and 'products' originated in Miami.

Both selling and serving a range of specialist fruit, Indian and Chinese teas, the shop is located in the heart of Marylebone Village and has none of the 'chintz' one might expect. Instead the interior combines the ethos of the American Zulu-inspired identity with the variety of infusions as divergent as Apple Amaretto Brew to Orange Spice Cookie and classics like Darjeeling, all reflected in the earthen palette and texture found in the scheme, balancing classical ideals with the formative contemporary products that the Levys are trading.

Devising the spatial sequence of three zones in the space: the Tea Wall, the Tea Station and the Tea Lounge (a comfortable seating area where purveyors can relax while teas infuse, enjoying the merchandise on offer) was an elementary departure point; the space pulls the visitor in from the smart London street in an uncomplicated, unassuming way.

Visually the Tea Wall is the *pièce de résistance*, boldly occupying the length of the boundary wall. It represents the simplicity of the uncrushed leaves with their vibrant earthy natural colours, celebrated in the mellow beauty of the architectural space, brought about by the physical material of the tea. The vessel that holds the individual teas is a cabinet with curved glass sealed openings which, in contrast to the tea itself, is a highly polished piece of furniture that adorns the space. Tea drinkers are aware of the cabinet before entering, as it is a dominant display that attracts the attention of passing pedestrians.

A large mother-of-pearl chandelier is the focus for visitors as, having strolled along the entry gallery, they locate the tea station and cake counter. A striking montage of mosaic encaustic tiles laid out like a magic carpet draws the visitor into the third zone, the Tea Lounge, where, once more, the colours of the tiles are taken from the 'weathered' appeal of tea leaves. In creating the architectural interior, an unorthodox teahouse has been made that plays on the illusion of tea ceremony rituals and the fantasy of a kitsch memory of British tea culture.

"Take some more tea", the March Hare said to Alice, very earnestly. "I've had nothing yet", Alice replied in an offended tone, "so I can't take more."

"You mean you can't take *less*", said the Hatter. "It's very easy to take *more* than nothing."[42]

PENDERYN

Nestled in the beautiful Brecon Beacons over a natural spring, the Welsh Whisky Company's Penderyn Distillery is one of the smallest distilleries in the world, and the only one in Wales. Welsh whisky—or *wysgi*—made from barley, wheat and honey, had been produced from as early as the fourth century, but ceased at the end of the nineteenth century. Then, on St David's Day 2004, the Penderyn Distillery opened, and Welsh whisky ran from the stills, available to the world once more after more than a century of absence.

Following a successful launch, the distillery decided to build a venue where public could watch the process of making the distilled liquor and provide a backdrop for tasting events. Archer Humphryes was commissioned to design the building after being approached by Welsh Whisky Company director Nigel Short, also owner of Browns hotel in Laugharne, famous for being the preferred drinking establishment of poet Dylan Thomas.

Creating a visitors' centre in a National Park was a mammoth undertaking for the architects, requiring unwavering perseverance. The process took several years, as they acquired an intimate knowledge of the landscape, which they visited frequently. The centre was officially opened by the Prince of Wales on 26 June 2008, and received huge critical acclaim.

"Do not go gentle into that good night. Rage, rage against the dying of the light."[43] A poem by Dylan Thomas inspired the buildings unyielding architecture, almost "raging" against the vale of greenery. Black stained, whaney edged sawn oak panel cladding gave the building a robust and impressive dissolute presence in the vale of the landscape.

The entrance continues the bold solution and is set against a dark matt background, a visual motif directly borrowed from the whisky bottle label and replicated here in brass and slate creating a *tableau vivant*. A light double-height entrance lobby is the start of the atmospheric space. "A seam of Welsh gold" corresponding to the amber of the whisky, and a background colour "black as coal" persist throughout the entire project as an emblem for the interior, a *mise-en-scène,* connecting spaces in the same way the streams flow through the landscape around the distillery. As the exterior is timber, so the interior spaces are lined with sawn timber, with a hand painted finish for a more refined, smooth appearance.

Whisky barrels and the Madeira casks, or *barriques,* used for the whisky's final maturation, are incorporated into the interior design as a memory and reference point. Stacked to act as space dividers—guiding visitors through the space to a tasting bar—their monochromatic, cylindrical forms and graphic notations are a counterpoint to building's austere organisation. The caskets add depth and rhythm to the vertical walls and continue the refined use of timber in the interior spaces. The tasting bar is made of black Welsh slate with a gold seam inlay, displaying an array of visual ornamentation characterised by the whisky bottles filled with amber coloured 'spirit'. The design provides views from the tasting areas into the still, bottling area and cooperage store, allowing aromas to be drawn in, absorbing the rich bouquet from the whisky and sherry soaked casks used to add extra flavours during the ageing process.

Archer Humphryes won many awards and accolades for the project, including a Royal Institute of British Architects award. This was all made possible by the client's investment and continued commitment to their exquisite products, described by Jim Murray in the *Whisky Bible* as "a superstar whisky that gives us all a reason to live" and "a prince of a Welsh whisky".[44]

In the landscape, the shiplap black oak cladding of the distillery is irregular in comparison to the rigorous, smooth, machined timber of the interior. It aids shadow and contrast when the sun hits the facade in this remote, isolated position in the Cynon Valley.

Penderyn is located on the southern border of the Brecon Beacon National Park. Cynon River flows through the site, water being a significant determinant for the position of the building where an abundance of pure water is required in the distilling science.

Home of the only Welsh whisky, a gold seam running through black coal is the emblem for the project, mirroring the river cutting through it, and usefully providing the contrasting palette of rugged sawn timber, smooth gold metal and zinc cladding, and the folded seamed roof for the visitors centre.

Engineered black metal doors with
linear polished brass pull handles make
a visible vertical where, otherwise,
horizontality is the predominant idea
to the external cladding arrangement.

Unpunctuated external walls of
dissolute black dominate in the
verdant landscape, revealing the
industrial usage of the project.

Minimal decoration allows the bottles
on the back bar to be unobstructed in
front of the smooth painted, timber-lined
interior. A solid block, the bar counter
with a gold seam of Penderyn folded
across its surface, echoes the unabashed
solidity of the building as a whole.

Signage upon entering the location continues the raw components of the composition of the building's exterior and interior—Welsh slate being the material selected for the obelisk marker.

In the tasting room, the barrels are useful divisions in the space and remind the occupier of the purpose of the visit. Reflected in the shiny surface of the gold, the black and white monochromatic graphics of the caskets are repetitive in their circular pictorial text.

DIOMED VILLAS

Diomedes was a prominent figure in the Homeric epic, a brave and valiant warrior who was well known in the Adriatic. According to Homer's *Odyssey*, following the capture of Troy he returned to Argos, one of the easiest and happiest returns from war. Then, met by the conspiracy incited by the revengeful Aphrodite, he fled. There is no clear legend on his death: the traditional line is that he mysteriously transformed into a deity within the sanctuary of the island off the Croatian coastline, now known to be close to the site where the Diomed Villas are positioned.

Facing the sunset west of the azure sea, the Diomed Villas are embedded into a rocky coastline. Close by, fragments of a temple and pottery adorned with Greek graffiti reading "ΔΙΟΜΕΔΙ ΔΟΡΟΝ"—"Gift to Diomed"—have been found. *Where* they have been found has indirectly contributed to the Cult of Diomedes, as these fragments place the area as a possible site for the mythologised Cape Ploče, on the Hyllean peninsula.

Conceptualising the nine villas in the cascading promontory, to a backdrop of the Homeric legend's maritime association, was the first accomplishment. The second, for Archer Humphryes, was working with the overriding planning constraints of coastal setbacks, plot proximities, gradient guidelines and highway infrastructure to satisfy local government, where new permits for development directly above the shoreline are non-existent. Fortunately, the site had a pre-existing permit for development dating from a decade earlier that the client was able to re-activate and apply to this new usage. This had to feature in the architects' new proposals for submission, owing to the fact that archaeological finds had resulted in fresh legislation protecting the coastal landscape. Geographical sensitivity was the prevailing order of the architectural language conceived for the project, along with the precision of the concrete structure, providing a deep, cantilevered terrace and 'picture windows' hanging at a similar gradient to that of the cliff.

After being granted permission to proceed, the initial prerequisites for Archer Humphryes were to achieve full sea views, a sense of privacy from adjacent properties, a combined balance between the cantilevered superstructures of the villa buildings, anchored rooms, gardens carved from the natural topography of the rock and subterranean spaces for parking, while avoiding extensive earthworks on the site—a limitation set by the permitting authority. A master plan was generated, carefully balancing individual villa positions with adjacent structures. An overarching principle was where to place openings for internal drama and at the same time create a rhythm along the coast alternating between natural terrain, inserted gardens and the structures of the nine properties. Responding by interspersing the villas into the coastline in this way is illustrative of the holistic approach that Archer Humphryes take to masterplanning, architecture, interiors and landscape design. Whilst each villa maintains a clear singularity, as an individual design has been produced for each one when considered as a group, the collection of nine villas creates a unified visual expression that is coherent and interrelated.

The use of crystalline render with fragments of mica and facing stone from Salona creates an envelope for the *moderne* form with generous terraces punched into the layout of the exposed freeform concrete frame above the podium level, and frameless glass balustrades affording an uninterrupted 'infinite' view. Recessed elements of the architecture are accented with incarnadine red—from Australian River Red Gums—and encaustic tempera plaster finishes, both on the exterior and within the villas chambers. Deeply rooted in ancient culture, red was reserved for walls facing west, seen here in the Diomed Villas' cantilevered terraces; facing the sunset, following the cardinal points of symbolism and fire. Red entry doors in Eastern and Western civilisations indicate stability and safety within the confines of the architecture; in the same way that the mariners worshipped Diomedes to provide their passage, the architecture unfolds intuitively in the interior spaces, with the public rooms taking the prime views. The interior, overall, is comprised of pure white spaces and white furniture, lightening the residences and allowing the blue of the sky and sea to be the primary aesthetic focus. Private bathrooms in black marble have walled gardens for external bathing.

Pools have infinity edges lined in pristine white limestone with rubble masonry, a contrasting imperfection in line with the rustic quality of the natural rock of the cliff. The stone work forms the edges of the cascading gardens, framed with walkways, external showers, lavender beds, planted olive trees and pergolas with arbors; pathways lined with bright fragrant flowers draw you to the to the shoreline, where traditional polychromatic boats, the designs of which have been in existence for millennia are moored at small jetties.

Diomedes was not only a civilising hero; he was also, more importantly, a protector of trans-Adriatic shipping. Perhaps without his shrine the peninsula would be radically different today, not offering the sanctuary for the villa's locale. "She sent him a warm and gentle wind, and Lord Odysseus was happy as he set his sails to catch the breeze. He sat beside the steering oar and used his skill to steer the raft."[45]

Stepped terracing provides intimacy and privacy to each individual villa, whilst the open pools give spectacular infinity views of the Adriatic Sea. Garden design is organised to give seclusion and sunlight, taking advantage of the vertical orientation, nestled in this Mediterranean terrain.

Cantilevered slabs are designed to form an external room enclosure with intense incarnadine red picked up under the rendered concrete soffit, which is timber-lined. A permanent *brise soleil* assists in heat gain where the fully glazed facade to the bedroom slides open, free from columns on the window line, avoiding break lines in the glass structure.

THE BEACH SAMUI

Heading to the titular beach in Thailand could be reminiscent of the filmic story that seeks out a Western Asian utopia as a paradigm for pure hedonism, or a Robinson Crusoe-style adventure in finding an idyllic beach untouched and without tourism.

In fact, it is a civilised paradise, with the village of Thong Krut overlooking a marine park, coconut groves and abundant resources. The name Samui is mysterious, encompassing many interpretations—one being *Mui*, the Malay word "Saboey" meaning safe haven. Chinese and Muslim fishermen were the first inhabitants of Samui; even today the bright coloured vessels sit on the turquoise waters juxtaposed against the red coral lagoon, part of the necklace of islands of Moo Koh Ang Thong, the national marine park.

When Archer Humphryes was appointed, the client was creating a retreat with 21 suites and penthouses. The Beach has been designed "to invite you to sit back, soak up the scenery and rediscover life's simple pleasures" whilst looking out over the Gulf of Thailand.[46] The architects were not simply invited to recreate a resort; their challenge was to create a lost Eden where environmental protection was of the highest priority. It transpired that their remit was to create a sustainable, visually stunning and colonial-inspired property that would complement the beachfront's natural beauty. It took courage to realise this project, set within the Marine Park; notably, the weather and erosion of the beach with substantial technical constraints had to be overcome, at the same time preserving the vast variety of abundant flora and fauna. Other considerations that were rigorously undertaken included factoring designs for natural windbreaks, natural shading, secluded terraces and future tree planting to make the resort invisible from the sea, at the same time allowing direct unencumbered ocean views from the interiors.

As so often in their work, the architects drew inspiration from local culture and traditions. The outcome is an architecture that has the scale of a house, allowing ocean breezes to ripple through the coconut palms with a structure resistant enough to withstand the awesome fury of a tropical cyclone. Indonesian Green Sukabumi sandstone, with its iridescent lustre, has been used for the architectural exterior as it is a thermally stable stone whose colour echoes the greens and blues of the sea and sky, with bronze accents in the design details.

With panoramic glass windows, Thai joinery reminiscent of local weaving, red lacquer doors capturing the colours of the formerly commonplace colonial Chinese fisherman's pots, with state of the art energy-efficient solar panels and naturally filtered water, the architects and the community have taken action and responsibility for their environment, creating an equal focus in working towards sustainability for the future. An open timber lattice extending the full height of the building is covered with Bougainvillea—which has a delicious scent—and within the grounds are Frangipani trees that add a lurid infusion of colour.

Elsewhere, the architects have created an atmosphere of discretion and lightness, with private outdoor tubs, muscle-soothing rain showers, and opportunities to float gently in the panoramic infinity pool or dine on organic island produce. Guests are invited to enjoy the intoxicating Thai fragrances and watch the fishermen miles out to sea, as they alight upon a spot where relative paradise has been regained. Yoga can be practised; the client, being an enthusiast, has encouraged private areas dotted across the complex for meditation. Assisting with the attainment of pure equilibrium, the architectural order responds to the geographical context and the harmony of the relationship between internal and external spaces.

At the Beach Bar, the option of being open on all sides was the architecture's guiding principle, achieved via cast bronze screens which can be adjusted to keep out the island breezes, or to allow them to circulate freely. A long, dramatic white marble bar appears to be carved from the floor, with brilliant Murano chandeliers delicately suspended above, fulfilling the theatrical aspirations of the client. A design classic, the Panton chair, sits comfortably in the Oriental interior with a lotus flower encrusted in the surface, something the architects created for the fiftieth anniversary of Panton for the Saatchi Gallery.

Archer Humphryes was also commissioned to come up with the character of the interior and furniture design. Again, they have succeeded in expressing an interior that is imbued with natural luxury, the notion of being barefoot with only the azure of the horizon to ponder upon. Each suite is lined in white washed timber; floors are laid in poured white terrazzo, which sparkles like the perfect white sands with washed up coral. Colour is introduced via cushions and wall coverings with bright reds, yellows and blues echoing the landscape of the red corals, the emerald sea and the Thai fishing boats sitting along the shore line.

Thus Paradise is not lost. "A paradise is within thee", marked by the moonlit evenings in Thong Krut where one could imagine purifying the soul as ancient Thai traditions have practiced for centuries.[47]

THE BEACH SAMUI

The near-untouched destination of the Angthong Krut National Marine Park is breathtaking in its southern location of Koh Samui, where few buildings exist, making the opportunity to create the architecture for The Beach even more challenging for Archer Humphryes.

Colourful Thai tail boats tied to sea grape trees are used as fishing vessels and are part of the community that surrounds this new 'design hotel'. Keeping all the indigenous fauna and foliage was a priority in placing the building, discretely located into the beachside. Yellow floral garlands, Phuang malai, kept for good luck, will adorn the lacquered red guest doors on the door handles as offerings for a welcome stay and can be seen adorning the boats.

Palm tree fronds in a fan formation, a sea of violet and red urchin shells to be found in baskets in the local market, protected red coral *corallium rubrum* in the surrounding marine park and tiny white bougainvillea flowers surrounded by colourful red bracts provided an abundance of visual information for the architects to advance their initial ideas. These include using Green Sukabumi sandstone in the scheme for elevation cladding and pathways, using vibrant colours of the bougainvillea flowers to the street elevation, shrouding the building in natural fauna, and using a fan shape in the signage for the project.

Here the rational orthogonal order of
the architecture—a white concrete slab
with Sukabumi cladding—is shaded by
coconut palms; bougainvillea flowers
trail through the lattice-work.

An infinity pool in emerald green, lined with the Indonesian green tiles, merges continuously with the sea of the Gulf of Thailand, wrapping around the restaurant. Here an unexpected polished black and white marble floor of the restaurant in a black border sits glamorously within the immaculate architecture stone details and expressed concrete structure.

Solid marble high table in Carrera marble forms
a bar counter, yellow sunset crystal chandeliers
following its length looking out to the bay on both
sides, moving from the restaurant to the pool, a
floating jetty that takes guests to the yacht launch
for candle-lit trips by moonlight to neighbouring
islands creates a sequence of scenes that take your
eye always to the horizon.

In the bedrooms, a cool modern interior is accomplished with verandas leading to external bathing areas with banana leaf candle lanterns for night-time light; waxed cotton drapes cocoon the room for intimacy. Tongue and groove ceilings in sea green are added to soffits of all rooms creating a beachside appearance. Authentic Thai craft is transformed into sleek bleached oak with matching cane backs, porcelain white stools from Chang Mai, a sparkle of Silver Kylin, link the interior and architecture seamlessly.

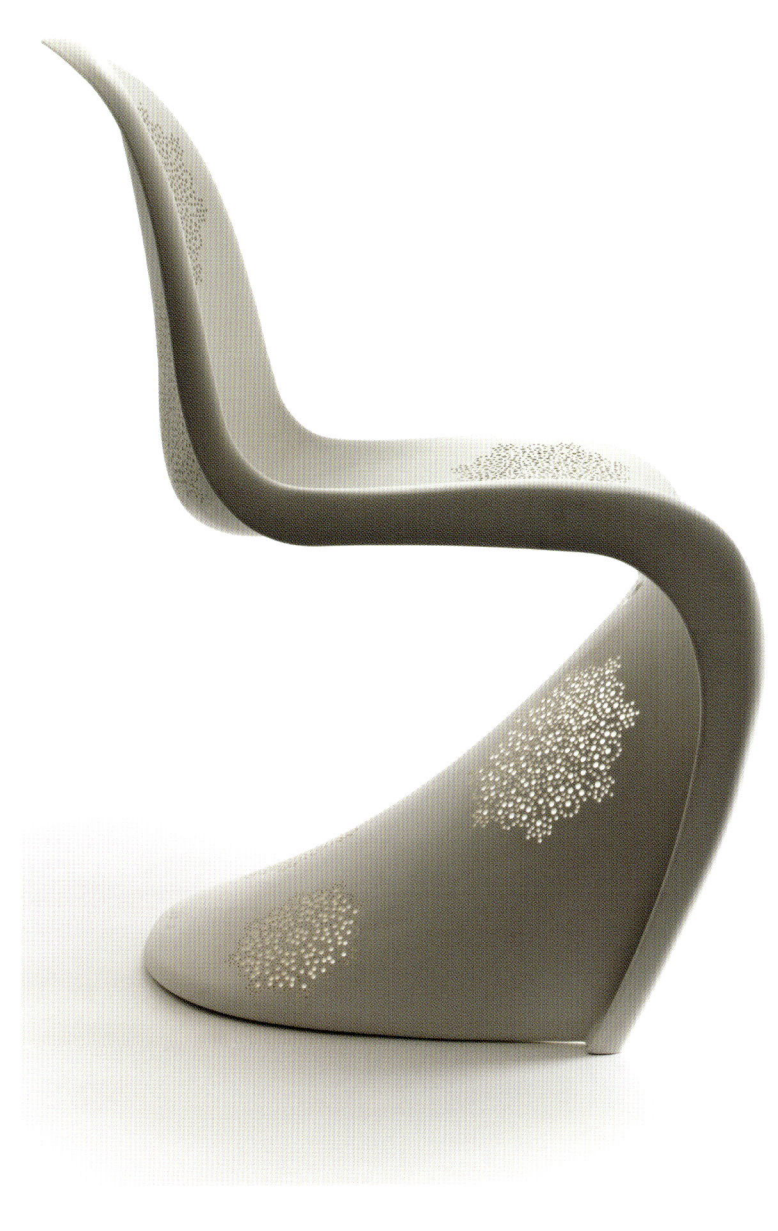

The first plastic moulded chair to be manufactured in the world, Vernor Panton's 'S' chair is an iconic masterpiece. To celebrate its fiftieth year, Vitra and the Saatchi Gallery invited Archer Humphryes to produce a customised version of this famous piece. Drilling an abstracted chrysanthemum pattern motif—which they artistically made and defined—into the 'S', the resulting chair received critical acclaim and formed a limited edition production for The Beach restaurant.

ARUBA

Surviving seaside piers are industrial structures that remind us of the achievements of Victorian engineering. The site for the Aruba bar and restaurant on Bournemouth pier, with its panoramic views of the English coast, was an incredible position to acquire along this seven-mile stretch of sands, one for which the client had waited patiently.

In 1841 only a few hundred people lived in the seaside village of Bournemouth. Rapid development began after the physician, Augustus Bozzi Granville, the author of a book called *The Spas of England,* which described health resorts around the country visited in the same year: "Bournemouth combines, to an eminent degree, the character of beautiful and sheltered rusticity with that of an open seaside residence… a formidable resort rival." He made several recommendations such as "to admit a few pleasure boats, and a short pier *sans prétention* yet convenient for landing on the beach".[48] George Rennie, the engineer, built the pier, which was opened in 1861.

Having begun with West Beach fish restaurant, one of the south coast's most celebrated eateries, Andy Price—a 'genuine Bournemouth boy'—set about with Archer Humphryes the difficult task of imagining "Aruba at Pier Approach". When the sun is shining in Bournemouth, the best place to be is on the beach and, initially, Aruba had the working title 'Sandy Feet' reflecting its direct access onto the sands.

Housed in a distinctive circus tent-shaped structure, the restaurant was to become a beach haven destination; the practice used its technical knowledge to overcome planning law in the seaside context. Elements of the project include a sun terrace with spectacular vistas, an island cocktail bar, al fresco and indoor dining as well as a private dining area perfect for parties or meetings. Evenings see part of the space used by some of the best DJs and musicians with a dance floor at the side. All of this was achieved in a vast open space of almost a 1,000 square metres, making it the biggest event space along the southern coastline.

Wishing for a 'holiday' atmosphere the client wanted an "Aruba Caribbean vibe", achieved by introducing playful swing seats, snugs, sunshine hot colours and exotica. Inspired by Cinquante-Cinq, unashamedly the place to see and be seen in the South of France (since Brigitte Bardot sipped a drink in the ramshackle hut whilst filming), the bar with its polished zinc top is the epic centrepiece, its astonishing 40 metre length seating 40 people. Tropical palm trees flank the bar and ripple in the breeze.

Painted tongue and groove boarding in the interior is reminiscent of Victorian bathing boxes and the colourful beach huts seen above the high tide mark along Bournemouth Sands. A mural of a mariner's chart of Poole Harbour has been added to the ceiling in one of the seating areas where sliding doors open onto the terrace. Outdoor showers have been included, with a view to creating a feeling of being in a resort. Tactile activities, such as washing the sand from your feet on the terrace whilst looking across the bay, create the appeal of the restaurant during the day, along with the full sweep of the bar's south glazed elevation. Whilst, at night, the renovation maximises the building's scale where 400 people can sip cocktails dreamily swaying to the music beneath the palm trees.

Further enticing the guest to relax are the textures and materials specified in the design of the furniture and lighting. Dining chairs with starfish and scallop shell emblems cut into the timber seats create a pictorial reference to the British coastline, with handmade wicker basket lanterns taking inspiration from the eighteenth century pleasure boats collecting sea urchins. Eclectic storm lanterns combined with suspended exotica, created by the architects (with the single exception of Moroccan lanterns being the client's wish, adding personal memories of travels) are interspersed with silvered mirrored balls for sparkle in this modern 'pleasure garden'.

Augustus Bozzi Granville concluded in his nineteenth-century book of spas that "Bournemouth is the realisation of a desideratum".[49] In Aruba, the architects have continued the spirit of the 'urban resort', by embracing the incongruous language of the Caribbean spirit whilst retaining the powerful irreverence of the traditional British seaside.

In an incredible location on the Victorian Pier, 'sandy feet', the working title for Aruba, was entirely reworked by the architects to create a venue that hosts 400 people daily throughout the summer in this beach bistro. George Rennie, engineer for Bournemouth Pier, remarkably built the engines for Archimedes, the world's first propeller-driven steamship. His listed structure presented a real challenge, and has succeeded as one of the most popular destinations on the South Coast.

Seaside pastels taken from Victorian timber beachside huts; Pistachio Green, Citron Yellow and Lulworth Blue created the palette for the interior. A sailor navy and white swing chair with knotted rope nestled amongst hurricane flask lamps and paper white lanterns are a reliquary of *object trouvé* that imbue the notion of being on vacation.

Aqua glass cabinetry for the back bar is reflected in the mirror above the fireplace where a conch shell reminds you where you are. Cement encaustic tiles in the same pastel colours as the tongue and groove timber wall finishes, and interspersed with starfish come from Provence. Carved into the cafe chair is the silhouette of a scallop shell, which sits under a maritime map of the Bournemouth sands.

MAISON TROPICALE

Working on behalf of hotelier André Balazs, Archer Humphryes Architects were responsible for overseeing the construction and installation of the Maison Tropicale on the South Bank in London as part of the Design Museum's exhibition Jean Prouvé—The Poetics of the Technical Object in the spring of 2008.

The structure played a major contribution to mid-twentieth century architecture and design. It presented a comprehensive introduction to Jean Prouvé's innovative, technical approach, and an impressive overview of his complete design oeuvre, including his collaborations with architects such as Le Corbusier, Pierre Jeanneret, and later Candilis, Josic and Woods, Maurice Novarina and Oscar Niemeyer.

The story of Maison Tropicale started in the late 1940s when Prouvé, a French architect and designer, created a prefabricated aluminium house in response to a housing shortage in France's West African colonies of Congo and Niger. With blue glass port hole windows to protect against intense sunlight of the equator, movable sun screens, verandas to optimise shading and natural ventilation, the building was designed to be environmentally responsive as well as easily shipped and assembled in a tropical climate.

When the project was conceived, architecture was perceived as a way of bringing about social transformation. While this idea merged with the concept of universalism, a modernist belief that an architect could create a space that could meet human needs and function equally anywhere, it was borne out of an age of imperialism and colonial rule.

Made from folded sheet steel and aluminium, the building did not resemble the local context, materials or building technologies passed down from generation to generation. Not surprisingly, the local people of Brazzaville and Niamey considered it an "alien" object. For ease of transport all the parts were flat, lightweight and could be neatly packed into a cargo plane.

Having fallen into a state of relative dereliction over the decades, Maison Tropicale, one of three prototypes, was salvaged and returned to France in 2000, where it underwent careful restoration. It was then displayed in Paris, rather fittingly outside the Pompidou Centre, and then in New York at a spectacular site on the East River under the 59th Street Bridge. It was here that André Balazs saw it, describing it as "love at first sight", and subsequently purchased it at auction at Christies.[50]

From the flat packed elements, arriving from New York via Paris after restoration, without drawings or photographic aide memoir of all the components, Archer Humphryes had to collate, draw and photograph the house in its dismantled parts. Similar to archaeological fieldwork where you discover and attempt to work out how the jigsaw should come together,

afterwards was generated a drawing and photo legend allowing the house to become a moving museum across the world, constantly assembling and disassembling with ease. This is what the architects achieved for the clients and future museums that will host the iconic masterpiece.

Meticulous detailed cataloguing of the structure prior to the houses' shipment to London was an incredible opportunity to revisit a historic building with modern forensic scrutiny. Archer Humphryes made it possible for the house to sit on the banks of the Thames. The house over time otherwise would have become damaged through incorrect assemblage from the lack of documentation and instruction, ultimately jeopardising the initial investment of saving it. The architects further assisted with a suitable location and orientation for the light to be dramatically flood the interiors. It was a pleasure for Archer Humphryes to contribute to the installation of Prouvé's Maison Tropicale at Tate Modern, a project which introduced his innovative work to a whole new generation.

What was of special interest to Archer Humphryes Architects was how most of Prouvé's concerns with the environment and mass production are still very much prevalent today, but were encapsulated by this modernist masterpiece more than 60 years ago. The only difference in its recent public displays is the absence of the tropical climate. Viewers to the restored Maison Tropicale are therefore exploring the project detached from its original purpose. But perhaps this break from the past allows a new understanding of Prouvé's genius.

"Jean Prouvé invented British high-tech architecture", said Design Museum director Deyan Sudjic. "He shaped the careers of Richard Rogers, Norman Foster and a generation of others."[51]

Among those was Renzo Piano, whose Shard stands today at London Bridge Quarter not far from the Maison Tropicale's temporary London site, where Archer Humphryes are now working with new clients to create an exemplary working community in the glass powerhouse. Like the modest house was in Brazzaville, Piano's skyscraper is highly incongruent to its surroundings, its high-tech form expanding on the technology first laid out by twentieth-century modernists. Piano's link with Prouvé began with the iconic Pompidou Centre in Paris, which he designed with Richard Rogers after winning a competition with a jury chaired by Prouvé. Piano and Rogers overtly wanted to break from the rigid idea of museums and an "intimidating myth of culture".[52]

Like Prouvé before them, they attempted to transform urban design through architecture, after all "The Maison Tropicale became an exemplar of a modern standard type house. The functionality, rationality and standardisation that characterised the project, make it an icon for industrial modernisation."[53]

A unique expression of a radical architectural vision, the prototype house was manufactured in France before export to Congo, fabricated from sheet metals whose raw materials were—ironically—imported from West Africa. Looming above its temporary position is Scott's Bankside Power Station with its 200 metre-long, steel framed, brick clad monolithic form and a central chimney standing 99 metres above the ground. Bankside was commissioned in 1947, two years earlier than Prouvé's experimental industrial metal Maison Tropicale, and received local opposition to its construction in equal measure.

MAISON TROPICALE

The adopted structural vocabulary is tubular or rolled sheet metal, welded and folded, which permeates the building enabling it to be lightweight. A double roof structure was designed to give natural ventilation in the building's originally intended position of the wet tropical climate of Brazzaville.

Verandas with adjustable aluminium sun-screens were incorporated chiefly for the long wet season, with the use of elements such as louvers, vents and screens responding to the climatic conditions. Unlike the raised platform in front of the Tate, originally the building was intended to sit on a beam-bearing structure mounted on piers. The interior—a combination of solid panels, sliding panels, portholes, doors and a tropical hardwood strip floor—is an array of defracted colour carefully controlled to diffuse the equatorial sunrays.

Having disappeared into obscurity after Brazzaville became independent, the building's phantomatic structure was rediscovered by the French furniture dealer Eric Touchaleaume when he visited Western Africa in the 1960s. He purchased all three 'Maison Tropicales', dismantled them, shipped them and turned them into collectable *objets* purchased at auctions. The installation at Tate Modern redefined the Maison Tropicale from a colonial pre-fabricated panelled house to an iconic museum piece, a status which resonates with Tate as a background—another building closed and decaying until it was rescued by an international architectural competition which gave new life to the structure as a modern gallery.

Dominated by inner walls perforated with a repetitious grid of blue glass portholes set on fixed and sliding panels, the interior is protected against ultra violet light. Jean Prouvé's Standard SP chair (Siège en Plastique) is still in production today, 75 years later.

Bankside chimney's height was limited to less than that of St Paul's Cathedral, which stands directly opposite on the north bank of the Thames, framed in the view from the Maison Tropicale's blue portholes.

HARLEY PLACE

A film and advertising director approached Archer Humphryes having been inspired by the practice's neighbouring Harley Street project. Initially, the clients envisioned creating an urban sanctuary for their frequent visits to London in contrast to their 'coaching' house in the Savernake Forest. What had inspired them from Archer Humphryes' portfolio was the monochromatic backdrops with carefully edited details combined with lighting effects that created scenic transformations to set moods. Understanding panorama, depth of expression and ability to control tones were the objectives of the design from the start.

Dreaming up a visual story utilising light was the key principle of the project. Generally, mews houses have a single aspect, and it was important from the outset to top light the property to filter light through three levels. Whilst filmmaking is about the big picture and the story, architecture is about the choreography of three-dimensional space and the perspectival depth of field. What both film and architecture rely upon is the manipulation of light in similar ways. In the words of the director Ingmar Bergman, when describing his thematic and aesthetic richness in building up ideas and panoramic vistas with light: "When we experience a film, we consciously prime ourselves for illusion. Putting aside will and intellect, we make way for it in our imagination. The sequence of pictures plays directly on our feelings. And film is mainly rhythm; it is inhalation and exhalation in continuous sequence." [54]

Visiting someone's home is an intimate experience. A sanctuary away from a main residence is a complicated idea. Whilst a home distinguishes us, regardless of location, people and places are engaged in a continuing set of exchanges. In this instance, the 'home away from home' was conceived as a 'city fantasy', almost allowing the resident to take a cue to live differently— momentarily—before returning to their home in the forest. The script is a familiar concept: the clients wanted a departure from what they had painstakingly created for themselves already as a home without any duplication and, at the same time, wanted to be astonished by a visual tranquillity that absorbed all their daily rituals in the mews house. As architects, Archer Humphryes were able to disconnect from the clients' private lives and, rather than borrow, recreate or isolate the clients' everyday thoughts, were able to generate the thrill of a separate identity for the project. This was the real task.

Within the brief was the proposition of retaining the character of the listed facades of the traditional mews with its stable doors, and to remodel the interior within the constraints of the eighteenth-century template, as the planning laws prohibited other approaches. The brick facade was painted in a traditional London 'railings' colour to enhance the picturesque nature of the traditional Georgian street and the new sharp joinery detailing maintained the nature of its traditional use.

In an area that has a strong historical identity, after exploration, the old interior was stripped away and an entirely new structure was inserted to create a three-storey void enabling the light to cascade into the new triple-height stairway. In this aperture the cantilevered marble stair hovers against—without touching—a glass wall separating the living space. The staircase was the fundamental aspect of the scheme and initially caused debate with the structural engineers as to whether or not it could ever be achieved. Careful analysis by the architects and the clients' unwavering dedication to the proposal eventually achieved the theatrical drama intended in the design.

The elemental material palette of the living space combines white and grey plaster, Carrera marble with white and grey veins, transparent glass, warm walnut and stainless steel. Each texture articulates the individual spaces of the house, all being anchored around the sky-lit vertical staircase void. Abundant natural lighting and artificial lighting provide different sensory responses to different aspects of the interior. Absorption of the light by the materials selected for the scheme assisted in the impression of succinct spaces.

The master bedroom situated on the top floor has a scale that is more enveloping. The upper floor houses the bathing experience, which is interlocked within the design of the bedroom and stair. Smoked glass, voluminous enclosures and skylights heighten the experience.

The ground floor has a different scale, providing an almost self-contained environment for the children or guests of the clients to drop in. Technological systems allow glass to become opaque for privacy, to soften the sound of the metropolis with sensors seamlessly and intelligently incorporated into the highly functional living home. At the entry, one is aware immediately of the aperture and the marble stone staircase overhead, pulling you upwards.

Furnishings reinforce the serene quality of the space and sit effortlessly with the clients' art collection. Daylight, night light and twilight transitions are complemented by the furniture collection and the way in which the client inhabits the spaces.

What the architectural design has enabled the clients to do is to possess the space and make it their own. To form new memories in the scope of their lifetime in the physical environment, to choose to be 'tourists at home at the weekend', or simply to 'live'. Through the imagination of the architects and their interpretation of the brief, this is what the backdrop of the mews house has enabled.

Ascending the stair, concealed lighting illuminates the white structure of the ceiling which takes its keynote from a best-liked Ben Nicholson painting relief. Theresa Green is the only colour introduced, which links the space vertically to the hallway in this Harley Street apartment.

A concealed square light source varies the ubiquitous white tones; a token newel post from the Georgian staircase is retained protruding in the original lime and lathe plasterwork as requested by conservation officer; the Castiglioni 1960s classic Taraxucum pendant using 60 incandescent light bulbs is the centrepiece.

White horizontal staggered glass brick tiles and opaline white glass walls sit above the datum of the lemon yellow glass recessed with hidden ambient light providing useful surfaces for bathing. Reflective mirror at the higher level forms a band around the bathroom creating full visibility for getting ready for a day at the office. Pure white Thassos tiles from Greece form the bath surround and solid floor slab, chosen for its crystal content.

Natural light pours through carefully conceived slots emphasising the suspended structure of the stair in the glass reflection. In contrast the top floor of the house is bright; white panels with an incision for opening the doors avoid projecting handles. The blond oak floor separates the bedroom and closet from the bathing areas that are formed with stippled stone.

Striations of light are absorbed onto the polished plaster. Here the Carrera marble treads float above as you ascend the walnut steps below to the living spaces on the first floor. On the top floor, smoked glass surrounding the shower mirrors the bedroom in its surface. Panelling in blond oak and simple joinery complete the material palette of the house.

In this room on the first floor, the living room is arranged around the fireplace set within the flush walnut wall that runs the length of the apartment culminating in the kitchen design. Here the cantilevered marble stair hovers above the ground floor entrance, the first tread being half a ton. It does not touch the glass partition, where there is a minute gap, defying the structure and weight of the treads touching the plaster party wall.

A lounge, hidden behind the Georgian facade of the mews, is a blend of artificial cuts of horizontal and vertical light. Skylights and diffused light from the garden add to the combination.

Walnut panels, solid walnut bookcase, walnut floor and walnut flush doors link the house front to back and dutifully provide a modest kitchen that suits the family's way of eating and relaxing. The dining table and chairs, similarly in walnut disappear into the background; a white table top was selected to accentuate the horizontal planes that define this interior.

A relief of textures that is at once soft, hard, glossy, matt, honed, reflective and luminous assists in bringing a uniformity to the house.

Deliberately not tapered, the
stair was created as a solid mass
of cantilevered stone, in a regular
pure geometric form.

HARLEY PLACE

THE SHARD

Archer Humphryes Architects' hotel design experience helped secure the practice a plum commission to create two floors of innovative workspace within The Shard in London.

A progressive approach to office planning was required as the project presented a great opportunity to work in a building that, as the tallest skyscraper in Europe, has had a huge impact on the capital's skyline, an emblem of the city itself.

The client, The Office Group, provides design-led, adaptable workspaces and has a track record of occupying inspirational buildings, including David Chipperfield's Gridiron Building at King's Cross and Richard Seifert's 1960s tower at Euston Station. Joint CEOs of the company, Charlie Green and Olly Olsen, describe their product as being "for people whose lifestyle cannot compromise on work space and who place high value on a world class address and being part of an inspirational environment".

At The Shard, the brief was to provide a home to at least 30 individual companies from the creative, media and technology sectors, creating 33,600 square feet of distinctively designed workspace on Levels 24 and 25, reflecting the diversity of this collective environment. The ambition for the space was both to complement the building's iconic architecture and to appeal to an emerging generation of entrepreneurs. These are people who expect their workplaces to be original with an anti-corporate mentality that reflects their lifestyles by blending work and play with the buzz of human connection, competitiveness and gossip. The design therefore needed to have an energetic vibe akin to that found in chic hotel lobbies in order to attract the sort of people who want to make visible the notion that they are 'hanging-out' rather than working as a regular 9 to 5 employee. An additional, and challenging, technical aspect to the design was that it needed to be flexible enough to tailor workplaces to personal needs.

Over recent years, working from home looked set to become prevalent and the office obsolete; however, these creative workforces crave community spirit and a busy, engaging hub. There is increasing evidence that productivity is sparked by removing yourself from the comfort of 'home'; Archer Humphryes excel at capturing the design vigour of a vibrant 'happening' place. Unlike the office blueprints of the 1980s and 1990s, the architects have not deployed gimmicks, such as table football, beanbags or fairground slides. Instead, the space epitomises informal glamour and imagination whilst, at the same time, is a serious spot for information-gathering and work production.

The Shard's irregular parallelogram floor plates forced a radical departure from orthogonal spatial planning. Instead, Archer Humphryes took inspiration from the shapes of abstract paintings by Ellsworth Kelly and Patrick Heron for the hierarchy of the internal spaces. The practice clad the core and concealed functional services such as utilities, a pantry and a phone booth and more private areas within the concentric 'cheeks' of the core, flanked by open-plan public areas, all with uninterrupted views out from all angles.

The northern aspect provides the reception, club, shared working, informal meeting, seminar rooms and a lounge bar, which is combined with a traditional library. These directly address the city and river views, giving the more social parts of the workspace the most dramatic views—St Paul's Cathedral, the City, the Tower of London and the longer river corridor. A trapezoidal walnut form and a rhythmic ribbed purling ceiling accentuate the 'collective areas' of the design and fan out to the more rarefied private office rooms.

A new staircase between Levels 24 and 25 provides a vantage point to appreciate the views as well as an opportunity for exhibitionism and chance encounters as colleagues ascend, descend and loiter. This staircase's location away from the communal core was a particular engineering challenge, and required a multidisciplinary rethink of the complex fire strategy for the entire skyscraper.

As well as designing the chance for social encounters, the workspace takes account of the requirement for withdrawal, privacy and thoughtful reflection. These areas are carefully planned where the exterior facade steps backs and a quiet open space can be found in discrete corners hovering in the sky above the London Quarter below.

The cellular offices are predominantly east-, west- and south-facing where the views have less to distract the mind, and were painstakingly positioned to respond to changing light levels during the day. A great deal of consideration was paid to the lighting. Since no new treatments to the angled facade panes were possible, a clever lighting design was required to diffuse the large contrasts between interior and exterior due to the expansive glass without internal blinds or curtains.

Like the hotel spaces Archer Humphryes is known for, the mood of the workplace is designed to be transformed over the course of the day so that at night the meeting area, the cafe area, even the flexible office spaces can become a magical bar perched over the Thames.

Throughout, a material palette was chosen to add warmth and familiarity to the space, including walnut floors with diagonal chrome edges. Fixed and moveable glass partitions—opaque, clear or with alternate graphic manifestations, with polished stainless steel mullions—reflect views inward and outward, while back-lit, fixed reeded glass panels are used to bring light into the circulation areas. Furniture is chosen to fit with the scheme's geometry, and for visual impact including pieces designed by Archer Humphryes, Carlo Mollino, Eero Saarinen and Frederick Scott.

Curvaceously arranged around the central core, the spaces on Level 24 of The Shard allow a continuous uninterrupted space to be created, connecting offices to the 'social' spaces of the scheme. 360 degree vistas are available throughout the rooms, providing the best views of London in the capital.

Walnut trapezoidal ceiling sculpturally frames the view creating visual interest in this widespan vista when entering level 24 at reception and carefully directs artificial light where required without the need for any ubiquitous fluorescent lighting.

Entrance way from the elevator lobby arrival. The backlit reeded glass provides an ambient light in the only area where there is borrowed natural light within the lift core.

Ribbed glass diffuses light in areas where the
natural light is diminished from the sheer depth
of the floor plate providing a ambient soft glow.
A suspended stair gives transparency and allows
the light to permeate the social areas.

City of London skyline appears, ever changing, like a silver gelatin theatrical backdrop print.

Reflective table surfaces add gloss and shine to the matt upholstered Knoll Saarinen dining chairs. Suitable for informal meetings, wireless working and coffee conversation.

'Lobby living room' are located on the north facing riverside of The Shard with spectacular sunsets in the evening, enlisting the atmosphere ideal for after work 'sundowners' and accidental meetings. Mirrored vertical fins are part of the architectural divisions reflecting light. If you want to cocoon yourself away for a deadline, the perspective on the shiny surfaces allows voyeuristically to see who is discreetly arriving in the space.

Glass manifestations to the graphic composition of the interior. They still allow oblique views of the interiors and continues the idea of lines of sight through the architectural.

Rhythmic walnut strutted ceiling was carefully connected to the vertical partitions like a flexible skeleton in a skyscraper which is permanently in motion. Tall buildings frequently move up to a metre in each oscillation like a rooted tree and is part of the structural response to horizontal wind forces.

Seminar spaces can be subdivided for individual
meetings or fully opened up for an event.
Importantly, this space is directly connected to
the 'lounge' and overlooks all the landmarks from
the Tower of London to the Houses of Parliament.
A monochromatic black and white palette allows
participants to communicate their own narrative.

Board room feel for sumptuous adaptable spaces with key views looking at the Dome of St Paul's. A corner office suite with glass entry doors and a curved opaque wall to the adjacent occupant can support a single business from one to 12 occupants.

Classic Fred Scott task chairs from the 1970s in black leather and engineered chrome accentuate the quality-conscious work culture and echo the mirrors and stainless steel fins of the partitions.

The cafe chair developed in solid walnut with black leather was manufactured by Fratelli Boffi and was designed as an informal meeting chair by Archer Humphryes.

Hot colours follow the contours of the building and deliberately mimic the aspirational age of aviation and travel in its concept. The height and scale of the building outstrips the adjacent skyscrapers and leaves the impression of floating in the clouds far removed from the busy intersection of London Bridge station terminus below.

Mirrors have been constructed beneath the descending dramatic stair. They endlessly reflect the London light which changes throughout the day, often capturing magnificent sunsets and provide useful vistas for greeting visitors awaiting in the lobby.

Archer Humphryes' muted blue sofa design is teardrop
shape responding to the reception space which you
enter from a variety of concentric walnut passages, as
you navigate yourself around the building's central core.
Sunset makes everything glow red and golden, ablaze
with evening low light a perfect antidote to complete
the day before the panoramic city lights twinkle.

Stainless steel circular balustrade rods add to the light weightless appearance of the staircase which is structurally hung from the floor above Level 25. This way the office could have its own independent connection without disturbing the tenant above and below the demise of the workspace. Walking down the stair, which is positioned for the best view of all fosters an interaction that goes beyond the basic brief and activities on the entrance of Level 24. This was important to create an energetic hub on arrival before ascending more private spaces for serious business.

On a raised platform to create a hierarchy of sight lines and independence from the main room, the general seating area embraces the work culture here—dining, drinking, reading, thinking, watching and talking take places. Giving the members the opportunity to converge or separate within the environment, seating arrangements give differing ergonomics for different situations and personalities. A trapezoidal ceiling design acoustically softens the sounds which allows for intimates conversations.

A lone sea green Saarinen 'womb' chairs beneath the
treads of the stair stands out against the full mirrored
wall. Perfectly contrasting with the muted grey, moss
greens, dusty pink and hot red upholstered fabric chairs,
the main space is an ideal place to sit and absorb the scene.

Endnotes

1   Liebling, AJ, "A Good Appetite" in *Just Enough Liebling: Classic Work by the Legendary New Yorker writer*, New York: North Point Press, 2005.

2   Rowland, Ingrid D and Thomas N, Howe, eds, *Vitruvius. Ten Books on Architecture*, Cambridge: Cambridge University Press, 1999.

3   Saint, A, *London's Architecture and the London Fire Brigade 1866-1938*, 1981.

4   Debord, Guy, *The Society of the Spectacle*, Ken Knabb, trans, California, Bureau of Public Secrets, 2014.

5   http://www.gnhlondon.com/our-rooms/cubitt-room. Accessed 28 April 2015.

6   Adam, Robert, *Ruins of the Palace of the Emperor Diocletian at Spalatro in Dalmatia*, 1764.

7   Steele, Bret, "The Master of Modern", *Port Magazine*, 14 November 2011. http://www.port-magazine.com/architecture/the-master-of-modern/. Accessed 28 April 2015.

8   iSalone blog, 8 April 2014, http://blog.isaloni.it/?p=1855&lang=en. Accessed 28 April 2015. See also Parissien, Steven, *Adam Style*, Phaidon, 1992.

9   Campion, Charles, *London Restaurant Guide*, London: Profile Books, p 471.

10 See Tracy, Nicholas, *Nelson's Battles: The Art of Victory in the Age of Sail*, London: Chatham Publishing, 1996. (Source credit: National Maritime Museum, Greenwich, London, Greenwich Hospital Collection.)

11 Quilley, Geoffrey, "The Battle of the Pictures: Painting the History of Trafalgar", in Cannadine, David (ed.) in, *Trafalgar in History: A Battle and its Afterlife*, London: Macmillan, 2006.

12 Sennett, Richard, *The Fall of Public Man*, New York: Norton, 1992.

13 Pavie, Auguste, *Pavie Mission Indochina Papers (1879–1895)*, *Volumes I–VII*, Bangkok: White Lotus Books, 1999. See also Pavie, Auguste, *A la Conquete des Coeurs*, Paris: Presses Universitaires de France, 1947.

14 Bowker, John, *The Message and the Book: Sacred Texts of the World's Religions*, London: Atlantic Books, 2011. See also The Churning of the World, The British Museum Collection, 2007, 3005.7.

15 Restaurant review, *Time Out*, 15 December 2010.

16 Baudelaire, Charles, The Painter of Modern Life and Other Essays, Jonathan Mayne, trans, London: Phaidon Press, 1995, pp 420–422. See also Charvet, PE, *Baudelaire: Selected Writings on Art and Artists*, Cambridge: Cambridge University Press, 1981.

17 Murakami, Haruki, *Q84*, Jay Rubin, trans, London: Harvill Secker, 2011, p 111.

18 Restaurant review, *Time Out*, 25 September 2015.

19 Grenz, Stanley J, *A Primer on Postmodernism*, Grand Rapids, MI: WM Eerdmans Publishing Company, 1996, p 89. See also Nietzsche, Friedrich Wilhelm, "On Truth and Lies in an Extra-Moral Sense, *The Viking Portable Nietzsche*, Walter Kaufmann, trans, London: Penguin Books, 1977, pp 46–47.

20 Andersson, Benny and Björn Ulvaeus, "One Night in Bangkok", Chess, RCA Records, 1984.

21 Maugham, Somerset, *The Gentleman in The Parlour*, London: Vintage Classics, 2001.

22 ibid.

23 Williams, Zoe, "Busabai Eathai, Bicester Village, Restaurant Review", *The Telegraph*, 30 October 2011.

24 Harding, Chris, "Restaurant Design: Superior Interiors", *The Guardian*, 21 October 2011.

25 Yau, Alan, alanyau.cn/ Accessed 28 April 2015.

26 Tibbits, Tim, "Food For Thought by Chef Tim Tibbits", *The Freeport News*, 24 January 2014.

27 Harding, Chris, "Restaurant Design: Superior Interiors", *The Guardian*, 21 October 2011.

28 See also Barnett, Richard, *The Book of Gin: A Spirited World History from Alchemists' Stills and Colonial Outposts to Gin Palaces, Bathtub Gin, and Artisanal Cocktails*, Grove Press 2012

29 The Gourmet Society Review.

30 Malevich, Kazimir, *The Non-Objective World: The Manifesto of Suprematism*, New York: Courier Dover Publications, 2003, p 78.

31 "Recipe for Success", RTE One Television.

32 Merrick, Jay, "Piano Hits the Wrong Notes: London's New Central St Giles Complex is Striking But Bereft of Joie de Vivre", *The Independent*, 3 June 2010. See also: Jodidio, Philip, *Piano: Renzo Piano Workshop 1966 to Today*, Cologne: Taschen, 2009.

33 ibid.

34 Piano, Renzo, *The John Tusa Interviews*, BBC Radio 3, 28 July 2004.

35 Farrow Design, "Plenty of Colour", *Peyton and Byrne Identity*.

36 Moore, Rowan, "The High Rise of Coloured Buildings", *London Evening Standard*, 21 December 2009.

37 "Lalit Suri: A Multi-Faceted Visionary Par-Excellence", *The Times of India*, 10 October 2006.

38 Lalit Hotels Press. See also World Trade Centre Delhi, "About Jyotsna Suri".

39 *Literature of Travel and Exploration*, Volume 3: R-Z, Jennifer Speake, ed, Chicago: Fitzroy Dearborn, p 1163. See also: Tavernier, Jean-Baptiste, "The Peacock Throne According to Jean-Baptiste Tavernier", *Historic Delhi: An Anthology*, New Delhi: Oxford University Press, 1985, pp 345–346.

40 Das, Purbas, "Koh-I-Noor No Show in Queen Jewels Exhibit", *The Sunday Guardian*, 15 January 2012. See also Sen, NB, *Maharaja Ranjit Singh And Koh-i-Noor Diamond*, https://archive. org/stream/MaharajaRanjitSinghAndKoh-i-noorDiamond/MaharajaRanjitSinghAndKoh-i-noorDiamond_djvu.txt. Accessed 29 April 2015.

41 Sadler, AL, *The Japanese Tea Ceremony: Cha-No-Yu*, Tokyo: Tuttle, 1962. See also Gold, Taro, *Living Wabi Sabi: The True Beauty of Your Life*, Kansas City, MO: Andrews McMeel Publishing, pp 19–21.

42 Carroll, Lewis, *Alice's Adventures in Wonderland*, London: Collins Classics, 2014.

43 Thomas, Dylan, "Do Not Go Gentle into that Good Night", *The Poems of Dylan Thomas*, London: W&N, 2014.

44 Murray, Jim, *Jim Murray's Whiskey Bible 2009*, Wellingborough: Dram Good Books, 2009.

45 Fagles, Robert, trans, *The Odyssey*, London: Penguin Classics, 1999.

46 Press Release, The Beach Samui, Koh Samui.

47 Milton, John, *Paradise Lost*, Stephen Orgel & Jonathan Goldberg, eds, Oxford: Oxford World's Classics, 2008.

48 Granville, Augustus Bozzi, *The Spas of England and Principal Sea-Bathing Places*, London: Henry Colburn, 1841, pp 512–536.

49 ibid.

50 Nayeri, Farah, "Hotelier André Balazs Flaunts Tropical Jungle House in London", *Bloomberg News*, 8 February 2008. See also Etherington, Rose, "Jean Prouvé's Maison Tropicale in London", *Dezeen Magazine*, 28 January 2008.

51 Design Museum, "Jean Prouvé", 7 December 2007 to 13 April 2008. http://design.designmuseum.org/design/jean-prouve. Accessed 29 April 2015.

52 ibid.

53 Rossen, Isabella, "La Maison Tropicale: From Failure in Niamey to Masterpiece in NYC", 19 April 2013. http://www.failedarchitecture.com/la-maison-tropicale-from-failure-in-niamey-to-masterpiece-in-new-york/Accessed 29 April 2015. Botti, Andrea, "The Work of Jean Prouvé and its Influence on Contemporary Architecture of the Late 20th Century, MsC Dissertation, Edinburgh: Edinburgh University of Architecture and Landscape Architecture, 2012.

54 Bergman, Ingmar, "Introduction", *Four Screenplays*, New York, Touchstone Books, 1989. See also Pearse, Gregory and Maria Pearse, *Ingmar Bergman: The Darkness Before the Dawn*, Erland Josephson et al, eds, Cologne: Taschen, 2005.

Acknowledgements

Enormous thanks to all our clients who's support and friendship has made the last ten years possible, all of whom have had faith in our thinking, and who have been part of the evolution of the practice. Especially to André Balazs, Alan Yau, Linda Yau, Gary Yau, Harry Handelsman, Jeremy Robson, Norbert Winkelmayer, Andrea Fuchs, Lord Edward Spencer-Churchill, Stephen Pycroft, Trevor Osborne, The Portman Estate, Andy Dodd, Ask Developments, Nigel Short, Carlo Boffi, Simon Green, Helen Green, Alan Payne, Ronisi Cazeli, Hieu Vui, Philippe Starck, Busaba Eathai Group, Bryan Lund, Charlotte Melsom, Dr Suri, Keshav Suri, EPR, Paul Monaghan of AHMM and, most recently, Charlie Green and Ollie Olsen of the The Office Group, Guy Nixon of Go Native, Piers Slater of Reef Estates, Crosstree and The Standard Team.

Pamela Buxton, Jan Carlos-Kurachek and Edwin Heathcote are to be thanked for believing in the merit of the publication and for their enthusiasm for the body of work. Embarking on the production of the book whilst a substantive amount of work was still in progress was an imaginative task in communicating what the content would be in a predominantly photographic book.

Our book would not be possible without Keith Collie's artistic interpretation of our work through his eyes, having followed us from the very first completed work through to the current day on all projects. Contributions from all the other photographers, all of whom have equally captured the spaces poetically in their individual images, are commendable.

To our invaluable team in the practice who, over the decade, have technically accomplished the creative ideas tirelessly. Working in the studio and based in on-site offices, it is incumbent on them to deliver our architecture and interiors. This extends to specialist manufacturers who provide prototypes, to Kevin Helas who has worked for us on graphic packages in the studio, to the team at Artifice who initiated the idea of the book and, finally, a huge thank you to Jeff and QLUE's immeasurable support in painstakingly organising our thoughts and ultimately our photography for digital media. QLUE creates our web presence—which influences how we communicate what we do everyday—whilst the book explains how we arrive at doing things.

We dedicate to the book to our families, who endure our endless discussions centred on buildings, and the children in our world who bring delight and priority to everyday with mischief, making life magical.

AWARDS
2008–2016

2008   BD Interior Architect of the Year Award

2008   ELLE DECORATION British Design Awards
—Best New Interior (Print Room)

2009   RIBA Award (Penderyn Distillery)

2010   Bloomberg International Property Awards—Best Resort
—The Beach Samui

2011   Restaurant and Bar Design Awards—Multiple Restaurant
Award and overall winner in all categories (Busaba Eathai)

2011   BD Interior Architect of the Year Award

2012   Shanghai International Design Festival
• Golden Seat Architectural and Interior Master Award

2012   Perspective Magazine Awards—Best Exterior Architecture
& Interiors—The Beach Samui

2013   Perspective Magazine Awards—Best Exterior Architecture
& Interior—The Beach Samui

2013   International Hotel Awards
(Great Northern Hotel)
• Five Star Award in the category of Hotel Interior for UK
• Regional Award in the category of Hotel Interior for UK

2013   International Hotel Awards
(Sans Souci Hotel)
• Best Hotel Interior for Austria
• Best Hotel Renovation/Refurbishment for Austria
• Best Hotel Renovation/Refurbishment for Europe

2013   European Hotel Design Awards—Interior Design of the
Year in the Restaurant Category (Plum & Spilt Milk);
Great Northern Hotel selected as overall winner

2013   Great Northern Hotel commended in the hotel
category at the New London Awards in association
with the Mayor of London

2014   Condé Nast Johansens Awards for Excellence—Best New
or 'Back on the Scene' Hotel (Great Northern Hotel)

2014   Perspective Magazine Awards—Best Interior
—The Beach Samui

2014   Condé Nast Traveller awards: Best London Hotel
—Great Northern Hotel

2014   New London Awards in association with the Mayor
of London: Chiltern Firehouse

2015   Asia Pacific Development Awards for Thailand
(The Beach, Samui)

2015   Condé Nast Traveller Gold List (Chiltern Firehouse)

2015   Condé Nast Traveller Gold List (Great Northern Hotel)

2015   Thailand Property Awards—Best Hotel Interior
Design (Phuket)—The Beach Samui

SHORTLISTED FOR:

2013   BD Interior Architect of the Year

2014   Restaurant and Bar Design Awards—Fast/Casual
(Amanzi Tea)

2015   RIBA Awards (Chiltern Firehouse)

2015   Civic Trust Awards (Chiltern Firehouse)

2015   Independent Hotel Show: Best Design
(Great Northern Hotel)

DAVID ARCHER

BA (HONS) DIP ARCH ARB RIBA

David Archer was born in Haddington, Scotland in 1967, and grew up in Manchester. After graduating from Canterbury University School of Architecture in 1989 he went on to complete his studies at the Bartlett School of Architecture in London under Peter Cook. In his dissertation he concentrated upon two works. One explored the six churches of Nicholas Hawksmoor, and how liturgy denotes the plan of the building; the second, the Leicester University Building by James Stirling, looked at the emergence of the independent group and British Brutalism. David's real talent as a student was his ability to draw ideas and convey thinking to others, which he continues to do in architectural practice.

Before establishing Archer Humphryes in 2002, he worked with hotelier André Balazs in New York as head of design for AB Hotels, collaborating mainly with Antonio Citterio and Jean Nouvel. Projects included 40 Mercer in Manhattan, and the Chateau Marmont in Hollywood. This was the start of a collaboration between David and André that has progressed into symbolic hotel commissions in the practice.

He had previously worked for Hopkins Architects, and for Philippe Starck in Paris, working on the design of the Felix bar in the Peninsula Hotel in Hong Kong and the Delano Hotel in Miami. David Archer met Julie Humphryes in 1997 whilst working upon the design of Ian Schrager's hotel the Sanderson, with Anda Andreu. This project sparked the start of David and Julie's collaboration and precipitated the formation of the practice with shared interests in architecture. Gradually, they have built up a business concentrating on four core areas: hotels, restaurants, resorts and residences, that harmoniously integrate interiors and architecture in listed buildings and new architecture, winning over twenty awards and citations of excellence internationally.

David has forged long-term relationships with several key clients including restaurateur Alan Yau, creator of Wagamama. Together they have developed a unique concept of 'dynamic dining' that has successfully translated into a collection of much-imitated eateries including Busaba Eathai and Hakkasan.

JULIE ANN HUMPHRYES

MA (CANTAB) DIP ARCH ARB RIBA FRSA

Julie Humphryes was born in the UK in 1970. She read architecture at Cambridge University, matriculating in 1989. Colin St John Wilson was Head of School and Eric Parry, now a Royal Academician, was her personal tutor as an undergraduate.

Before returning to Cambridge to complete her studies in 2003, she spent time in Berlin at Studio Daniel Libeskind and in practice in Hong Kong, travelling extensively in the Far East. Julie submitted two theoretical dissertations whilst at Cambridge. The first was a study of the Mesoamerican site of Tikal in Guatemala with the esteemed archaeologist Professor Norman Hammond. This work focused upon historical complexes whose monumentality is hidden in the landscape. Julie's second piece of writing explored documenting works by Terragni, a pioneer of the Italian rationalist architecture in Italy and the metaphysical art movement of De Chirico and Morandi. It had been inspired by a thesis that she found in the architectural library by Peter Eisenman whose interests explored the history of the Casa del Fascio. Attempting to reconcile tradition and modernity has remained a fundamental principle in the practice as an approach to understanding ideas.

Julie's first project to be constructed was the Georgian Group Headquarters on Fitzroy Square. On completion of the project she worked with Australian architects, Denton Corker Marshall, as project architect on the Sanderson Hotel with Philippe Starck, before joining Virgin Atlantic. Here with Richard Branson's futuristic array of ventures she collaborated on the early designs of luxury travel projects with Airbus and Boeing, along with award-winning airport lounge interiors with Softroom and Eight Inc Research which took her to all parts of the world exploring luxury resorts and travel, being resident in Tokyo.

She was co-head of design at YOO, the residential and hotel design company set up initially by Philippe Starck with Matthew Freud as chairman. Until recently she directed the creative direction of the YOO Studio.

Julie is a Fellow of the Royal Society of Arts and has taught at numerous academic institutions including the Royal College of Art in London. David and Julie frequently speak at events and forums internationally and, most recently, with the World Monument Fund discussing Food and Architecture.

Essay Contributors

PAMELA BUXTON

Pamela Buxton is a London-based architecture and design journalist. After reading Classical Studies at Bristol University, she worked on a series of publications including *Designers' Journal*, *Design Week* and *Building Design*. Now freelance, she has contributed to many national newspapers, consumer magazines and trade publications including *RIBA Journal*, *Blueprint*, *Grand Designs*, *Time Out*, and *Wallpaper**.

She has also worked on the production of several design and architecture books for leading publishers including *Tony Fretton's Buildings and their Territories* (Birkhauser Verlag) and *Understanding Architecture* by Robert McCarter and Juhani Pallasmaa (Phaidon).

JAN-CARLOS KUCHAREK

Jan-Carlos Kucharek is currently senior editor of the *RIBA Journal* and editor of its sister title *Products in Practice*. He studied architecture at Canterbury College of Art and completed his Diploma at the Bartlett School of Architecture, UCL; gaining his Part III qualification as an architect in 2001 from Kingston University. Carlos spent five years working at Foster+Partners where he was involved on commercial projects in the City of London. After moving to the *RIBAJ* as assistant editor, he also worked part-time for Marks & Barfield, Hudson Featherstone, David Morley, WHAT Architecture and Fourthspace architects. He has written freelance articles for *Building* magazine, *Building Design*, and *AJ*, and spent a year as deputy editor of *Construction Manager* magazine. He was also a contributor to Sarah Wigglesworth's Routledge publication on her straw bale house, *Round and About Stock Orchard Street*. He has been on end-of-year crit panels at the Bartlett and AA Schools. He lives in north London.

EDWIN HEATHCOTE

Edwin Heathcote is the Architecture and Design Critic of *The Financial Times*. He is also an architect and designer himself and the author and editor of about 20 books including *The Meaning of Home*. He is a contributing editor to *ICON* magazine, has a monthly column in *GQ* and is on the editorial board of *AD* magazine. He is currently setting up an online archive of writing on design.

Photography Contributors

KEITH COLLIE

Archer Humphryes Architects started working with Keith Collie at the beginning of 2002. Keith studied at the Royal College of Art in London, and has spent his professional life working with many distinguished clients.

Keith's initial architectural commissions for Archer Humphryes included a mews building in Paddington and the Coach House at Court Essington. The resulting imagery not only gave the architects a record of the built work but, through Keith's lens, placed and interpreted the work within both an architectural and artistic context. Photographs are often partly or completely abstract; Keith's interests in architectural history, modern architecture and the city and his surroundings as well as his commitment to research and teaching throughout his career all enrich the visual record that he has been able to compile documenting the practice's work. All photography by Keith Collie unless otherwise indicated on the facing page.

JONATHAN IRISH

Jonathan Irish is a professional outdoor, adventure and travel photographer based in Washington, DC. He specialises in shooting active lifestyles, landscapes, and cultures abroad. His work has been published by clients worldwide, including *National Geographic*, *National Geographic Traveller*, *The New York Times*, *Outside* magazine and many others. Jonathan is also a board member of the American Society of Picture Professionals (ASPP), DC-South Chapter.

EDWARD TYLER

Professional photographer Ed Tyler has exhibited at the National Portrait Gallery and recently held his debut solo show in Shoreditch, London, based on architects and the buildings that have inspired them.

Ed studied at Edinburgh School of Art. He specialises in portraiture and loves nothing more than a European shoot with a great lunch thrown in.

NICHOLAS KAY

Nicholas Kay was born in London in 1986. At the age of 11 he moved to France, where he developed an early interest in photography. After graduating from the École Supérieure des Métiers Artistiques, he decided to specialise in studio photography, in particular, still life, fashion and portraits. One of his most acclaimed exhibitions was his real-life recreations of famous tattoos, for which he sourced all the items including daggers and roses. He is known for lighting, shooting and retouching everything himself.

TIM CLINCH

A photographer all his working life, Tim has lived and worked in London, Madrid, Cadiz, South West France and, more recently, Bulgaria and Eastern Europe. He works for a wide variety of magazines all over Europe and America, including *Condé Nast Traveller*, *Forbes Life*, *Town & Country*, *Food Illustrated*, *House & Garden* and *Traditional Home*, and has had many books published, including *England's Hideaways*, a guide to the best secret hotels and castles in the UK.

Tim's prestigious hotel clients include The Chiltern Firestation Hotel in London, The Faena Hotel+Universe in Buenos Aires, The Hotel Villa Magna, Madrid, The Chedi Hotel in Muscat, Oman and The Casa Claridge Hotel in Miami. He has been House Photographer for Michel Guerard's Les Pres d'Eugenie in South West France for several years.

JOAKIM BLOCKSTROM

Originally from Stockholm, photographer Joakim Blockstrom is based in London. Shooting spaces, still life and portraits he works globally for *Dwell, House& Garden, Wallpaper, Elle Decoration, Australia Vogue Living* as well as collaborating with some of the worlds most renowned designers and brands, Turkish Airlines, Cole & Son, Andaz, Lanesborough and ME hotels, YOO, Conran, Lexus to name a few.

In September 2014 Bloomsbury published his collaboration with chef Ollie Dabbous titled *Dabbous, the cookbook*, a beautiful art/cook book. Joakim has since 2011 been shooting and curating the Heirloom project, an ongoing collaborative exploration in objects we inherit and the stories we associate with them.

PHILIP SINDEN

British-based photographer Philip Sinden has worked for publications the world over, predominantly in the fields of fashion and environmental portraits. Publications he shoots with currently range across *British Vogue, Harpers Bazaar, Wallpaper*, Porter magazine, Wall Street journal, Hole and corner, Vanity fair, Net a porter, Saturday telegraph magazine* and *Condé Nast Traveller*, while his recent commercial clients include Landrover, Jaguar, Hogan shoes, The shard and Freemantle.

Project Credits

P 28

P 76

P 106

P 156

P 162

P 178

P 198

P 202

P 208

P 216

P 228

P 244

P 270

P 282

P 286

P 292

P 308

P 324

P 332

P 338

P 346

P 350

P 364

P 372

P 386

P 404

Project Credits

CHILTERN FIREHOUSE
AHA Project Team: Howard Jones, Laura Calistri, Jason White, Hugo Silvestrin, Polina Liarostathi
Client: André Balazs, Manhattan Loft Corporation
Landlord: Portman Estate
Contractor: Knight Harwood
Engineer: Rambol
Mechanical + Electrical: Rambol
Quantity Surveyor: Baqus
Acoustic Consultant: Sandy Brown
Lighting Design: Isometrix
Garden Design: Miranda Brooks
Historic Building Consultant: Donald Insall Associates
Graphic Design: Alexander Kellas Creative
Direction and Brand Design: Austria
PR: Mathew Freud
Consultant Chef: Nuno Mendes
Furniture Procurement: Hotels AB and Chris Garrod Global
Decorator: Studio KO
Uniform Design: Hotels AB, Elizabeth Saltzman, Emilia Wickstead, J Crew
Kitchen Design: GWP
Budget: Confidential

GREAT NORTHERN HOTEL
AHA Project Team: Andrew Burdon, Jason White, Howard Jones, Sol Negron, Zaheen Shah, Polina Liarostathi, Alejandra Chequin,
Client +Hotel Operator: Jeremy Robson and Ram Capital Partners
Main Contractor: Mace
Structural Engineer: Rambol
Mechanical and Electrical Engineer: Rambol
Lighting Consultant: FireFly Lighting Design
Quantity Surveyor: MPA
Building Control: HTS
Planning Consultant: CBRE
Historic Building Consultant: Giles Quarme
PR: Sauce Communications
Graphic Design: Here Design
Consultant Chef: Mark Sergeant
Specialist Furniture Manufacturers to Archer Humphryes Designs: Benchmark, Fratelli Boffi. Vickers and Rothschild
Kitchen Design: Charlie Parker
Computer Render Graphics: Miha Lah
Budget: £35 million

SANS SOUCI HOTEL VIENNA
AHA Project Team: Geoff Howard, Zaheen Shah
Client: Sans Souci Holdings with Norbert Winkelmayer
Operator: Norbert Winkelmayer with Andrea Fuchs
Local Austrian Architect: A2K
Furniture manufacturer: Walte: Siegrfried Walte
Computer Render Graphics: Miha Lah
Budget: Confidential

ADAM HOTEL CROATIA
AHA Project Team: Rob Mumby, Geoff Howard
Client: Spectator Group Solis
Local Architect Consultant: Ante Maric
Budget: Confidential

AFTER ADAM
AHA Project Team: Alejandra Chequin
Client: Fratelli Boffi and Archer Humphryes Architects
PR: R & W Design Brand Management, Milan
Graphic Identity: Kevin Helas

AYAA
AHA Project Team: James Engel, Geoff Howard
Client: Gary and Linda Yau
Contractor: Tekne Shopfitting Ltd
Engineer: Michael Hadi
Lighting Consultant: Jonathan Coles
Specialist Furniture Manufacturers: Cappellini and Barber Osgerby
Graphic Design: Made Thought
Budget: £1.6 million

NATIONAL CAFE TERRACE
Client: National Gallery/Peyton and Byrne
Tender Submission: Tekne Shopfitters Ltd
Budget: N/A

ISARN
AHA Project Team: Geoff Howard, Rob Mumby
Client: Tina Yau
Contractor: Lister Carter
Lighting Design: Jonathon Coles
Budget: £100,000

CÂY TRE
AHA Project Team: Rob Mumby
Client: Vietnamese Kitchen
Contractor: Tekne Shopfitting Ltd
Graphic Design: Kevin Helas
Budget: £150,000

NAMYAA
AHA Project Team: Rob Mumby, Matt Cousins
Client: Busaba Eathai Ltd/Alan Yau
Lighting Design: Isometrix
Specialist Furniture Manufacturers: Ben Dawson Furniture
Graphic Design: North Design
Uniform Design: Pocket
PR: Sauce Communications
Contractor: PBH Shopfitters Ltd
Budget: £1.6 million

BUSABA EATHAI GROUP
AHA Project Team: Rob Mumby, Zaheen Shah, Alejandra Chequin, Pedro Picado
Client: Busaba Eathai Ltd
Contractor: Tekne Shopfitting Ltd / Fileturn
Furniture Design: Christian Liagre and Archer Humphryes Architects
Lighting Design Concept: Isometrix
Graphic Design: North Design
PR: Jessica Salmon
Budget: Multiple Project budgets ranging from £550,000 to £1.5 million

DUCK AND RICE
AHA Project Team: Howard Jones, Laura Calistri, Matthew Foster
Client: Alan Yau

Concept: Autoban
Contractor: Pat Carter Shopfitting
Engineer: Rambol
Electrical: MCE
Mechanical: Summit Design
Quantity Surveyor: Michael Porter Associates
Project Management: Mark Alford
Graphic Design: North
Lighting: Light IQ
Budget: Confidential

PRINT ROOM AND INK BAR
Client: Andy Price
Project Team: Geoff Howard
Contractor: Michael Launder, Lister Carter
Computer Render Graphics: Lee Humphries
Budget: £2 million

PEYTON AND BYRNE
AHA Project Team: Andrew Burdon
Client: Peyton and Byrne
Contractor: Stanhope PLC
Graphic Design: Farrow Design
Budget: Confidential

SAVERNAKE HOTEL AND RESORT
AHA Project Team: Geoff Howard and Lee Humphries
Client: Buena Vista Hospitality Group
Executive Architect: Formation Architects
Engineer: URS
Quantity Surveyor: Gleeds
Mechanical + Electrical: Chapman Bathurst
Structural Engineers: Scott Wilson
PR: Communications Group
Golf Course Design: Peter Alliss Design
Marketing and Sales: Doreen Boulding
Kitchen Designer: Ken Winch
Budget: Confidential

LALIT HOTEL LONDON
AHA Project Team: Howard Jones, Rob Mumby, Geoff Howard, Zaheen Shah, Pedro Picado
Client: Lalit Hotels Delhi
PM: Gerald Eve
Executive Architect: EPR
Engineer: URS
Mechanical + Electrical: Hurley Palmer Flatt
Quantity Surveyor: Gleeds
Furniture Procurement: Chris Garrod Global and Lalit Hotels
Kitchen Consultant: Salix
Landscape Designer: Olivier Vecchierini, Know Design
Budget: Confidential

COURT ESSINGTON
AHA Project Team: Geoff Howard
Client: Andy Dodd and Ask Property Development
Contractor: Lister Carter
Budget: Confidential

BUXTON CRESCENT HOTEL AND GAINSBOROUGH HOTEL
AHA Project Team: Fleta Burbury, Geoff Howard
Client: Trevor Osborne Property Group

Spa Operator: Danubius Hungary
Engineer: Aecom
Historic Building Consultant: Nicolas Jacobs Architect
Budget: Confidential

AMANZI TEA
AHA Project Team: Geoff Howard
Client: David Elghanayan
Contractor: The French Group
Budget: £400,000

PENDERYN
AHA Project Team: James Engel, Geoff Howard
Client: Welsh Whiskey Company and Nigel Short
Contractor: Interserve
Engineer: Clarke Bond
QS: Faithful + Gould
Services: Saba Consult
Budget: Confidential

DIOMED VILLAS
AHA Project Team: Rob Mumby
Client: Spectator Group
Computer Imagery: Lee Humphries
Budget: Confidential

THE BEACH SAMUI
AHA Project Team: Rob Mumby, Zaheen Shah, Alejandra Chequin
Client: Absolute World Group & Design Hotels™
Brand Development: Charlotte Rose Melsom
Furniture Procurement: Rich Millar
Computer Digital Renders: Spoon Visuals
Budget: Confidential

ARUBA
AHA Project Team: Geoff Howard
Client: Andy Price
Contractor: Tekne Shopfitting Ltd
Lighting Design: Jonathan Coles
Budget: Confidential

MAISON TROPICALE
Client: André Balazs
Contractor: Tekne Shopfitting Ltd

HARLEY PLACE
AHA Project Team: Geoff Howard, Rob Mumby
Client: Simon+Helen Green
Contractor: Pat Carter Shopfitting
Engineer: Rambol
Budget: £850,000

THE SHARD
AHA Project Team: Laura Calistri, Howard Jones, Matt Foster, Eliana Stenning, Alejandra Chequin, Nikhil Dhumma
Client: The Office Group
Contractor: Modus
Cost Consultant: Quantum
Specialist Sub contractor: Tekne Shopfitting Ltd
Specialist Sub contractor: Canal (Staircase)
Fire Strategy: Arup

© 2016 Artifice books on architecture,
the author, contributors, architects, and artists.
All rights reserved.

Artifice books on architecture
10a Acton Street
London
WC1X 9NG

t. +44 (0)207 713 5097
f. +44 (0)207 713 8682
sales@artificebooksonline.com
www.artificebooksonline.com

Designed by Sylvia Ugga at Artifice books on architecture.

All opinions expressed within this publication are those of
the authors and not necessarily of the publisher.

British Library Cataloguing-in-Publication Data.
A CIP record for this book is available from the British Library.

ISBN 978 1 908967 27 5

Artifice books on architecture is an environmentally responsible
company. *Cool Contemporary Classic* is printed on sustainably
sourced paper.